From The Pit To The
Pinnacle

Conquer your depression in
20 minutes a Day and
Awaken your Bliss

I0151828

Richard Link

1st WORLD
PUBLISHING

From The Pit To The
Pinnacle

Conquer your depression in 20 minutes a Day and Awaken your Bliss

Richard Link

© Richard Link 2008

Published by 1stWorld Publishing
P.O. Box 2211 Fairfield, Iowa 52556
tel: 641-209-5000 • fax: 641-209-3001
web: www.1stworldpublishing.com

First Edition

LCCN: 2008935230
SoftCover ISBN: 978-1-4218-9016-6
HardCover ISBN: 978-1-4218-9015-9
eBook ISBN: 978-1-4218-9017-3

Disclaimer

The author assumes no responsibility for any injury and/or damage and/or loss sustained to persons or property as a matter of the use of this product's liability, negligence, or otherwise, or from any use of operation of any products, methods, instructions, or ideas contained in the material herein.

Disclaimer: *I am not a psychotherapist. If you need counseling for any health issues, you should consult your local professional or specialist.*

Table of Contents

◆

Introduction

I would like to introduce my newest book: *From the Pit to the Pinnacle: Conquer Your Depression in 20 Minutes a Day and Awaken Your Bliss.* Boldly revealing how everyone can feel pleasure, harmony, and happiness everyday, this is one of the most revolutionary methods of finally ridding your life of debilitating depression.

Mindeze has scored another major coup: finally, a way for everyone to start living the life the way it was meant to be lived. With our new home study course you too will feel the happiness, joy, and anticipation of living a full life every day! You will be able to release the depression from your life. Because everyone is different, there are no magic formulas; every person is special and requires different steps and processes, we help select the right steps for you. This may become a struggle for some, because you must meet head-on what the root causes of your depression are.

I explain what methods to use and I help you select the right course of action for your particular needs. Many of you will resist the first time or first several times. Keep trying. Go back and pull out the home study course to reevaluate where you are and where you want to be. Be absolutely clear on who and what it is you need to confront. By doing so, you will know what the best methods are for you to use to overcome your depression. At this stage, you can let yourself get excited in anticipation of finally getting depression out of your life.

Chapter 1

What Is Festering in Your Mind

---◆---

The party is in full swing. There is singing—dancing—laughing. Everybody is having a fabulous time. Food, booze, and great friends. Can it get more perfect? Yes it can! For some strange reason you find that you can't get into the celebrations. The belly laughs you once had cannot be ignited. Even cracking a smile is difficult.

You look for excuses: "It's my age." "Am I getting sick?" "Is it something I ate?" "I have not slept well." Ah that's it—lack of sleep. You accept your prognosis, because for the last month you were waking up three to four times a night, and for no reason it seems. So there will be no enjoying the party tonight.

Dark Clouds Looming

Thoughts that you have never entertained before present themselves on a regular basis, occurring when you least expect it and at the most awkward times. Suddenly, those hairy-legged spiders become monsters to fear. Heights at which you soared like an eagle before now paralyze you even at the thought of high places. Strangers are now avoided at all costs, because they are after you.

Sleeping, dreaming, being awake brings no escape. You feel you are in another place strange and horrible. It's too terrible to be real. You cringe as you are beckoned to take part in this psychotic drama. You are dictated to as to what scenes you have to play out. The distorted characters and personalities you portray are like real living people, but living inside you.

Chapter 2

UMO's-Unidentifiable Mind Objects

At times you can't put a name to the images that you start to harbor. The images take on a form of their own, they become real objects. Who are they? What are they? One after another they come bringing in their friends from unknown horrible places. The more you try to find out where they come from, the more they disguise themselves. If only they were friendly foe. Alas, they come in different shapes, sizes, colors, and sound at times worse than the present residents.

Strange Beginnings

Press the wrong button; rub the wrong vessel; key-in the wrong combination. You will then open the door to unstoppable monsters. Your feelings are now strangers to these uninvited guests. Your wires become switched, because now your feelings become your thoughts instead of your thoughts becoming your feelings. (See explanation in Chapter 3.)

This situation creates black holes that you start to plunge into. To be able to control this descent is not an issue—but survival is. You would do anything to climb out of this pit. But how? You feel that you are walking in a slimy swamp surrounded by pitch darkness, fearing that at any moment you may slip deeper into one of those black holes and be gone forever.

Chapter 3

Where Is This Coming From?

You receive countless bits of information during the day; even when you are asleep your mind is processing information. You receive a thought every second—that's 86,400 thoughts in a 24-hour period.

Your subconscious mind is the powerhouse where the realms of all possibilities reside. It accepts any thought that you feed it, whether it is true or false, real or imaginary. Considering that the subconscious mind is millions of times more powerful than the conscious mind, it sure packs a punch.

Sophisticated medical equipment has shown that brain chemistry changes in response to the different thoughts you have. At the same time, brain chemistry forms new neural pathways in the brain associated with specific thoughts. The brain then sees and recognizes these patterns and creates feelings in the form of emotions, which are finally expressed as behaviors in action. It is the rewiring of the brain circuits, by means of thoughts and changes in brain chemistry, that you acquire new habits or maintain the old.

I will give you an example. Let's say that you started thinking that if you were in an elevator, it could plunge to the ground. You then reinforce this with images of being in the elevator as its falling. You then bring in strong emotions of fear: you can hear yourself screaming and the sounds of the cables on the elevator snapping. You smell burning rubber— the smoke of electrical wires shortening—and sense your impending annihilation. You can actually feel perspiration running down your forehead, sweaty hands, dry throat, and heart palpitating. To your subconscious, it is very real. By constantly playing this scenario in your mind, the neural pathway for this thought becomes stronger after each input. It now runs on automatic. Now whenever you see an elevator or even think of one your fear of the impending danger causes you to panic with the associated physical symptoms. In fact, on many occasions you do not even have to think it.

If you are somewhere that resembles an elevator, the color of an elevator, smell of burning rubber or of electrical wires burning—or anything that you have allowed your subconscious mind to see as a pattern for this fear—it will automatically respond with associated unpleasantness. This is the reason why some people may make the following kind of remark: "I just get anxious for no reason and I don't know where my anxiety comes from." The subconscious is now operating on automatic. How can someone release and break this cycle? Keep reading.

Before you can actually release your depression, you need to know what it is; you cannot fight an enemy if you do not know who it is. Be absolutely clear on who and what it is you need to confront. By doing so, you will know what are the best methods to use to overcome your unfriendly foes. At this stage, you can let yourself get excited in anticipation of finally releasing depression from your life.

Chapter 4

Know the Mind of Your Enemy

Characteristics of Depression

You may be comforted to know that every normal person becomes sad or miserable at some time and will experience a low mood.

These experiences are similar in a number of ways to states of depression, but in depression the feelings are much more intense. Depression may be mild, moderate, or severe, and this will correspondingly affect the severity of the following characteristics or symptoms you will experience.

There is no one symptom that all depressive people have, and the following symptoms may not all be present. So please be aware of this. For example, even sadness may be absent.

Insomnia

When you are depressed you will probably wake early in the morning and unable to get back to sleep. Or you may wake intermittently throughout the night, or else lie awake for long periods of time—accompanied by racing uncontrollable negative and morbid thoughts.

Dejected Mood

In your conversations, the typical words you would use to describe your feelings might be one or all of the following:

Miserable	Lonely	Ashamed
Hopeless	Unhappy	Worried
Blue	Downhearted	Useless
Sad	Humiliated	Guilty

Your feelings may fluctuate during the day, or in cases of severe depression, may persist all the time.

Low Self-Esteem

If you are depressed, you will generally have a poor opinion of yourself and may say to yourself, "I'm no good…I can't do anything right…I don't deserve to live…I loath myself." These negative attitudes towards yourself may develop along with illness, or be a long-standing personality trait that has contributed to your illness.

Hopelessness

The gloom of your depression expresses itself in a loss of hope for the future. This is often focused on your illness itself making you believe that you will never recover and that there is no cure for you. It is often related to suicidal intent.

Loss of Motivation

You find it difficult to do anything that is demanding, and you are drawn to less demanding and more passive activities, which have fewer responsibilities. You would rather escape from your problems rather than cope with them.

You may find it especially difficult to get started on anything in the mornings, and your own self-will may be completely paralyzed.

Loss of Gratification and Interest

You feel a loss of interest in activities that you normally enjoyed and valued, whether it be work, leisure activities, or concern about your personal appearance and hygiene.

Loss of gratification may start with a few things and then, as your depression progresses, spread to almost everything else, including eating, sex, receiving expressions of love or friend-ship, conversation and social activities.

Crying Spells

You could experience increased periods of crying, which is common among depressed people; this is so especially with women. In mild depression, women may burst out crying, but it is unusual for men. In moderate depression, men who have not cried since childhood may cry while discussing their problems. Sometimes crying brings relief, but with some people it may make the depression worse. If your depression is severe, you may find it difficult to cry even if you want to.

Loss of Mirth Response

If you are depressed, you will find it difficult to respond to humor in the usual way and no longer be amused by a jesting remark, joke, or a funny cartoon.

Impaired Concentration

You will find it difficult to keep your mind on what you should be doing, and your thoughts drift away when you try to work, follow what people are saying, or even when you are reading and watching television. All your thought processes appear to slow down.

Change of Weight

When you are depressed you tend to lose your appetite and this leads to weight loss. Or, you may overeat to comfort yourself and so gain weight.

Exhaustion

Lack of energy is a very common symptom and indeed may be a dominant one for you. It may be associated with a general slowing down of movements. Sometimes you may have more energy as the day wears on, but in the morning you may feel you have no energy to do anything.

Guilt

Oversensitivity to guilt is a symptom of depression, and in severe forms you may blame yourself unnecessarily for things you have done or failed to do in the past. Pathological guilt is where these acts or omissions are only trivial in nature. Sometimes you may feel guilt about your present condition and your inability to "pull yourself together." Delusions about the "unforgivable" sin, or about other sins, may occur. You may believe terrible punishment is imminent, or even that you are the devil.

Suicidal Intent

While suicidal wishes occur in nondepressed persons, they occur far more frequently in the depressed person. You may feel a passive wish about suicide, for instance, "I wish I were dead," or an active wish, such as "I want to kill myself." It may occur as an obsessive thought or as a daydream. The importance of this symptom is obvious, and counseling is to be sought in both instances.

Hypochondria

Here you often have an excessive concern with the possibility of body illness; often it is concern about cancer or heart disease.

Hallucination

In more severe cases, and in some mild cases as well, hearing voices that condemn you is quite common. This may also involve seeing things, for example, animal faces in food, husband or wife in coffin, or dead people.

Stupor

In this severe condition a person is generally confined to bed. You are mute, inactive, and uncooperative, and needs attention in every way. You need to be fed, washed and bathed, and may resist all attempts at movement. There may be a lack of feeling, but on recovery, you often speak of the distress you have suffered.

Physical Symptoms

In this situation you may complain of vague and ill-defined pains in the head and the face that are very persistent, of indigestion of various kinds, constipation, feelings of weight in the stomach, a bad taste in the mouth, blurring of vision, and general weakness. When you are thoroughly examined physically, you present nothing that will satisfactorily account for your symptoms.

One of the outcomes of depression is that it may have caused you to grapple with some of the more serious matters and questions of life that you would have probably overlooked if you were in a more cheerful mood.

So my advice is that you grapple with the serious parts of life while you are feeling well and cheerful. You sure will get better answers a lot more quickly as well.

To know what it is you are up against is a battle already half won. Why? You now have the knowledge. To become the winner in this contest, you must gain coping skills, as well as, most importantly, a winner's ATTITUDE. Read on and find out how to get both.

Chapter 5

Black Holes and a Case History

As you have read about some of the universal causes of depression in the previous chapter, be aware that the causes of depression can be as varied as each individual mind. Prolonged states of stress and anxiety will produce emotional chaos. The degree of sensitivity for each individual will determine how soon the symptoms of depression will appear. It could be days, weeks, months, or even years.

It only becomes a matter of time when the onslaught begins. Let me give you an example:

John was a first-year teacher straight out from college. He was given a class to teach that comprised of boys aged 15 to 16. John could easily be classified as a "control freak." Every thing had to be as he planned. Things had to be in their proper place, work had to be completed on time, behavior had to be exquisite. There were no grey areas—only black or white. His high expectations matched his enthusiasm and talents. But at a price.

The ways you view the world is by means of your senses; you then interpret what you see and hear, according to your belief systems and how you reacted to previous experiences. You sum up what is true for you and at times, unfortunately, find it hard to change.

In class, if a student dared talk, or even turned his head around, John would immediately get upset. Emotions of anger, anxiety, and stress were not the only effects that he would have experienced.

Adrenaline would rush through his body, releasing all sorts of negative hormones, cortisone being one of them. Heart rate would increase, blood pressure skyrocket, and blood sugar increase—to name only a few physical effects. There was no escape. The fight or flight mechanism set in. This would produce a vicious cycle—his negative thoughts contributing to the chemical changes, which would further produce the physical symptoms.

John's flurry would amuse his students; boy, did they now know how to get a reaction from him.

Day in and day out, arguments followed. The stress would reach unbearable levels, its sister—anxiety—soon followed, trapping the poor teacher. It only took about three days before John found it difficult to sleep at night. This made him become very irritable during the day, which further aggravated the situation.

He soon developed high blood pressure: 145/100. His insulin levels were high enough to classify him as a borderline Type 2 diabetic. You can now see how negative thoughts in your mind produce physical ailments. John felt he had no way out. His ego did not allow him to walk away. If he did, he would consider himself a failure. John soldiered on—then after five months he started to feel some of the dreaded symptoms of depression. Panic, unknown fears, teariness, and even suicidal thoughts.

It was in this state that John came to me for a consultation. He felt embarrassed as he divulged his condition in detail to me. It took some time for John to start feeling relaxed and actually comprehend what I was saying to him. In our conversation we were able to identify his unrealistic expectations, especially in the classroom. John did not hesitate to accept my suggestion that we needed to release his pent up stress and anxiety. For I know through experience that in many cases, the symptoms of depression would subside if that happened.

By using muscle testing (which I show you in the course), I was able to find a point on his body—in John's case it was on the middle of his chest—which was associated with the negative events going on in his mind. This point indicated depleted energy, much like a blown fuse in an electrical circuit. I then instructed him to tap, rub, or hold that point while going over in his mind the stresses, anxieties, and fears he was experiencing. He was to do this for 20 minutes a day for the next week.

After a week he visited his doctor. Both were surprised to find that his blood pressure was very close to normal and his high blood sugar had significantly dropped.

Having now released his negative emotions, I then proceeded to reprogram his thoughts. I showed him the following procedure: By using muscle testing again (and using a priority mode using you fingers, which I show you in the course), I was able to find a point on his body that could be rubbed, tapped, or held for positive thoughts and emotions. For John it was just below his belly button. (An alarm point for the stomach meridian; this will also be shown to you.)

I than gave him some positive thoughts and emotions that were specific to him to instill into his mind. He was then to follow the procedure regarding the point as already described. He was to do this for 21 days, 20 minutes a day. Why 21 days? Some scientists believe that it takes approximately 21 days to form new a habit. My experience does confirm this to be the case.

Whenever, a negative thought entered his mind, he was to just say the word *delete* and think of pleasant things. OK—it did take some time and self-discipline to get used to following the procedure, but the rewards were well worth it. John finally had emotions that serve him.

John now sleeps throughout the night. He does not get nearly as upset at the slightest provocation. He has changed careers—no doubt wisely. And he does not experience any of the depressive symptoms he once had.

Of course there are people who are genetically predisposed to depression, as we are led to believe. In such cases they can still be helped by using my techniques.

The only criteria are that they persist with the program. This is simple to learn and implement. Visit http://www.mindeze.com for more information.

I have also noted that certain types of foods can bring on a depressive episode. Not surprising with all the artificial additives that are being put into our food and drink. Just look at what happens when kids at a party drink soft drinks. Some turn into little monsters! Of course some people are more sensitive than others to additives, so it's not surprising that depression is seemingly becoming an epidemic in our society.

I remember being in a restaurant with some friends. The

food was great, especially the tantalizing flavors of the different exotic sauces. It was only about half an hour after we had our meal that the complexion of one friend, Jake, took on an ash-grey color. Our concerns about his well-being were warranted, because he started to complain that he felt very dizzy and experienced chest pains, heart palpitations, extreme anxiety, and the gloom of depressed associated with fear. Heart attack, we all thought. Immediately we called for an ambulance. It arrived to our great relief in a matter of minutes.

The paramedics did every test, and assured Jake and the rest of us that he was not having a heart attack. The tests, however, revealed that he in fact was having an allergic reaction to something he may have eaten.

Intuitively, I ran back into the restaurant and asked the proprietor what kinds of additives they put into there food. He informed me they used a variety of additives to enhance the flavors, and that different dishes had different additives added to them. The most common additive was MSG—monosodium glutamate. I took a small sample of MSG and tested Jake to see if this was the offending culprit.

I did this by putting the MSG on his body (any part of the body). With one of Jake's arms outstretched I pushed down on his arm it went straight down (this is what is known as muscle testing)—that is, he could not hold his arm up while I had the sample of MSG up against his body. When I did not have the MSG on his body, his arm was able to resist as I again pushed down on his arm. By holding his forehead, getting him to breathe more deeply and slowly, and rolling his eyes around from left to right and vice versa, his symptoms disappeared. In all it took about ten minutes. After the incident Jake told me that he had suffered with depression in the past—and that while he was reacting to MSG, he experienced the same symptoms.

Chapter 6

My Story—From the Pit to the Pinnacle

---◆---

Depression one of the most debilitating, crippling conditions that one can suffer from. How and why some of us get depressed is still not completely understood. However, there are some reasons why we can be afflicted with this condition. The brain chemistry changes to some degree in people who get depressed. These changes cause the synapses to release certain chemicals that produce electrical conductivity. This forms a neural pathway that the brain then encodes into its memory bank as a response—in this case, depression.

I am a classic example of someone who has experienced deep, ongoing depression. Before it hit me, I was a happy person and satisfied with the way my life was going—my family, finances, etc. My mother lived in a "granny flat" at the back of our house and I would inevitably see and speak to her every day. If it were not me, it would be someone else in the family who would talk to her. She always had company. In spite of this, I noticed that there was something wrong. In fact, on reflection, she displayed depression for most of her life. She was very religious and displayed a firm faith. I have my suspicions (which she also confirmed) that it was her religious convictions that made life somewhat easier for her. After my father died in 1984, she lost the will to live and this showed in her negative speech and actions. She would always talk about her sickness (high blood pressure, cholesterol, diabetes, etc.) and a desire to die so that she could be with her deceased husband, family, friends, even strangers. I tried on many occasions to take her out and to take her on holidays with us.

At times she did go out, but she could not wait to get back home to sit in her room and pray or watch television. She just wanted to be alone. She had lived a hard but active life where her youth was taken away from her. She was a victim of the Nazi regime in Eastern Europe during the Second World War. She was literally dragged from her father's arms at the age of 15 and did not see him or her mother and sister until 40 years later. Her brother was shot dead and his body thrown into a river while trying to help her father who was being beaten by soldiers. She was then taken to a slave camp and later to a Nazi experimental hospital where she was experimented on but never found out what they actually did to her. It was here that she witnessed some horrific scenes that haunted her all her life. The most amazing thing was that she completely and unequivocally forgave her tormentors and even prayed for them. I remember her as a person who loved dancing and singing when she was young. She was full of love and extremely charitable, preferring to help her fellows rather than herself.

On many occasions she helped me financially when I was

down and out and always encouraged me in my own times of crisis. It was on a Saturday at the end of September 2005 that I was with my brother, Les, having a couple of relaxing drinks at the local RSL (an Australian association, Returned Soldiers League) around lunch time.

We were both very happy and I remember Les telling me that he felt something good was about to happen. After a couple of drinks I left and went home. When I arrived, I decided to visit my mother in her granny flat. It was about 2.00 pm in the afternoon. As I got to the front door I heard her groaning. I rushed in and saw her lying naked on the bathroom floor, as if she had suffered a stroke.

I simply froze. I immediately recalled her telling me that one day I would find her lying on the floor naked, dying. I felt all my emotions immediately freeze. It was a mixture of fear and surrealism. She had envisaged this scenario on many occasions over the years and here she was, exactly as she had pictured herself. The ambulance took her to hospital. Tragically, the doctors gave her little hope as she had experienced a massive stroke and was partially blind and paralyzed down her left side.

It was Wednesday, October 5, and I was working on a client when the phone rang at about 7.30 pm. It was my wife telling me that my mother had just died. I felt somewhat relieved that at least my mother had my wife and my daughter, Veronica, by her side when she passed away and that she would no longer be suffering. I rang Les and we both went to the hospital.

As we walked into to her room, my daughter and my wife were beside my mother's body. I then kissed my mother, as did my brother. She was still warm. My wife and daughter left, and Les and I were alone with her to say our farewells. I could not cry or express any emotions, which I thought very strange. As her body lay there, I lifted both her arms and laid them over each other onto her stomach. Again I went into a panic.

I told Les that this is exactly what my mother had instructed me to do when she died when I was only 4 years old. What amazed me was that I did this automatically. It was deeply programmed in my mind. When Les and I left the hospital we realized that she had died on October 5 at about 7.30 pm and that my father had died on October 17 at about 7.30 pm. It was as if she wanted to die at the same date and time, trying to make sure she went through the correct portal so that she would meet her beloved husband. We got into the car to drive home.

When I switched on the engine, the first song that was played, and which I have not heard for decades, was "Knocking on Heaven's Door." Les and I just looked at one another in awe, surprised yet comforted. We definitely felt Mum was trying to tell us something.

How I Overcame Depression

As a former teacher at a secondary school, I was no newcomer to stress. Teaching at this level is an emotional minefield as you are constantly under pressure to perform. Can you imagine standing in front of a class where 90% of the students don't want to be there, let alone pay attention to what you are teaching? Add to this the constant misbehavior, which drains you of all energy, and you have a formula for complete frustration. Constantly shouting and getting into arguments with the students undoubtedly causes your blood pressure to rise, not to mention your adrenaline level! When you are under this sort of pressure during every class, every working day, something has to give.

If you don't deal with it, both your physical and emotional health suffers. It was in this sort of environment that I found myself in when my mother had a stroke and died. I had found her lying helpless and naked on the bathroom floor. What was astounding is that she had predicted the exact scenario of her death and had told it to me. It was only after some deep reflection that I was able to make the connection between the bizarre emotions that I was to feel and the circumstances surrounding her death. At my mother's funeral I was simply unable to mourn her death. My emotions had become frozen. I could not cry and this made me feel guilty.

About two weeks after the funeral, I suddenly found myself wide awake at 2.45 am with some very strange feelings. I was experiencing an overpowering sense of fear. But fear of what? It certainly felt like abject terror—my heart was pounding and I was perspiring profusely. I even felt like screaming. I remember saying to myself "Here we go again!" as I had been in this situation before, but it was nothing like this. As I lay in bed, myriad bizarre thoughts rushed through my mind. They were mainly morbid, nightmarish images over which I had no control. The fear continued to build. My heart began pounding faster and faster and the perspiration increased. A vicious cycle had set in. What could I do? I eventually got out of bed. By that time it was 3.00 am and I felt like running around the streets screaming to get relief from this terrifying monster. I could not wait for daylight to arrive. I told myself that if I could survive until then, it would all go away. As I started to walk from my bed, I noticed that my balance was gone. Literally bouncing from wall to wall, I eventually managed to make it to the toilet. Walking from the bathroom and into the kitchen, an overwhelming fear came over me.

Was I having a stroke just like my mother? Was I having a heart attack? How would I function? I kept this ordeal from my family and friends. I did not want to dwell on what had happened, and thought that these feelings and symptoms would go away and my sense of balance return after a week. Unfortunately, the situation only got worse.

Everything started to annoy me. I would stay in bed and close my eyes but, no matter how hard I tried to stop it, the torment continued. When I finally got up, I stayed inside the house. I could not even go to the front door, let alone the outside gate. I felt trapped in my mind and this was expressing itself in my physical behavior. Going to the hotel to have a couple of drinks with my friends was out of the question. Shopping and socializing with friends or family came to an abrupt halt. All joy had left my life. I was left in a permanent state of sadness, anxiety, panic, and depression.

I began to feel like I was ready to fade away and die. Absolutely nothing interested me. I couldn't even laugh (and I have always enjoyed laughing). It was as if my personality was not my own anymore, as if some demon had possessed me. But if I was no longer myself, then who was I? I got a hint as to the answer to this question when some in my family commented that I was acting like my mother. It was as if I had taken on her personality.

I was negative and did not want to talk. I became like my mother even in my mannerisms. In retrospect, I realized that this was most likely because I did not want my mother to die and still wished her to be around me.

It struck me that I was comforting myself unconsciously by taking on her traits so that, in a way, she was still physically alive inside me. The thought of going out even to a family function terrified me; it was totally irrational but very real to me. My imbalance was another reason for not wanting to go out on top of the constant questioning: "What's wrong with you? Are you all right?" These inquisitions only caused me further anxiety. "Please leave me alone! You just don't understand," I would think to myself, feeling irritation.

The panic attacks were getting worse. At times I would literally run away or completely avoid certain situations or events because of the overwhelming fear as well as the physical symptoms of racing heart, perspiration, and feeling faint. After some time, I developed hypochondria. I checked my pulse constantly (which was consistently running at 100 to 120 beats per minute). I was only able to sleep for two to three hours every night, which made me extremely weak and irritable during the day.

I felt that the people around me just did not understand. It was as if I was in a closed cocoon calling out for help but with nobody able to hear me. At times I was told to "snap out of it." I felt resentful because I certainly did not want to be in this situation. If it were simply a case of flicking a switch, I would have done it long ago. The nightmare continued. I could not concentrate and the only thoughts I had were of doom and gloom. It was not long before thoughts of suicide began to plague me. It would be the easy way to end this suffering once and for all.

On many occasions my wife and I were invited to visit friends or to attend family functions. Normally I would have loved to go, but in my present state I simply could not. On one occasion my wife and daughter visited one of my married daughters. I stayed at home feeling totally despondent and thought that my wife might as well be a widow for all the attention I was giving to her. I felt sorry for myself. I sobbed and kept asking myself why I had to be like this. I curled up into a ball and could not even watch TV or listen to the radio. If I heard particular songs, I would be overcome with emotion. About eight weeks after the depression had started, the situation came to a head. I was presenting to a group of people when a sudden attack of sheer panic and anxiety set in. My heart was pounding; I was a ball of sweat and felt completely unbalanced.

I tried to stay on my feet but kept falling down, desperately trying to hold onto any nearby object that would help to stabilize me. I was gripped by a feeling of extreme weakness and despondency and sincerely felt that I was dying. I only hoped that the end would be quick. After a few minutes (which seemed like hours), I somehow found myself still standing. In front of me was the group of people I was addressing. They were looking at me in sheer bewilderment.

I ran out of the room, back to my car, and drove off. I remember saying to myself, "I have had this! This is it. I am going to seek help." I made an appointment with a doctor and was admitted immediately. I remember walking into the doctor's surgery and feeling as if I was walking on rubber. Everything seemed so strange. The doctor took my blood pressure, which was 170/90. This was extremely high. He took a second reading and it was a whooping 200/100! The more stressed I got, the more it went up. My blood sugar was way over accepted limits and I had palpitations. The doctor recommended that I take a cardio test. He took one look at my results and immediately sent me to hospital by ambulance. I felt completeness.

At the hospital I was wired up for another test and was told to just lie there. I had no choice but to relax. Every half hour my blood pressure was monitored and a sample of blood was taken. In the meantime, I was given a cup of tea and a sandwich and I started to feel better. Four hours later the doctor arrived at my bedside. He was looking very serious and asked me what I would like him to do for me. "What a strange question!" I thought. I told him that I wanted to be put on medication, antidepressants, blood pressure tablets as well as drugs for my high blood sugar. He looked at me, smiled, and said, "I am not putting you on any kind of medication. You don't need them." I was completely taken aback. He then told me that my blood pressure was now 130/90, which was passable, and that my blood sugar was fine. "It's all psycho-somatic," he explained.

I was stunned. I had no idea that my thoughts were so powerful that they could influence my physical symptoms that dramatically. To me, it was the first sign of hope. I was absolutely relieved to hear his positive diagnosis. Two weeks after the hospital episode, I still had depression. It would not go away. In fact, it was getting even worse. In spite of this, at the back of my mind was a feeling of hope. It was a strange combination! I visited my local doctor, who had my case history. He suggested that I go on antidepressants. I did not refuse him as I was willing to try anything. On the second day after taking the medication, I felt a lot worse. When I went back to my general practitioner, he recommended that I try a different brand. He said that there were 20 different brands and it was just a matter of trial and error until I found one that would work for me.

The second group of antidepressants made me feel even worse! They made me feel as if my mind were no longer my own, as if I had been invaded be an alien entity. I even thought of committing myself to a psychiatric hospital. The world around me was vibrating with madness and I could hardly walk. I felt unbalanced, disorientated, and in a complete haze. I wished I had something physically wrong with me because it would have been so much easier to cope with. Even eating depressed me as the food had no taste. I soon lost a lot of weight. I started to pray. It was the only thing left. The anguish and torment were unbearable. In this desperate situation, feeling alone and isolated from the rest of humanity, all I could do was to come to terms with and accept my condition. It was from within this lowest ebb that my mind had an insight into a potential solution. I had been involved in natural health for many years (specifically energy therapy). Depression is a disease that consumes your mind, body, and soul. You become incapable of thinking rationally.

You believe that there is nothing that can help. Somehow I rallied enough strength and decided to use my therapy (and other natural methods) to beat this monster. My elevated blood pressure, blood sugar, and heart palpitations had shown me the power of thought. Thought is energy and I sincerely felt that I was destined for recovery. Simply thinking of being well will not make you better, but it is an important component. It was not just my thoughts that contributed to the change in my brain chemistry. It was the disruption in my energy system combined with a broken spirit. EMT (Emotional Mindeze Therapy) and other energy therapies clear negative energy, unblock energy pathways so that energy can run throughout the body and mind unrestricted. Once this is achieved, the body and mind can heal themselves.

I did not hesitate. I stopped taking the antidepressants (luckily, in my case, with very few side effects) and started to introduce the right nutrients into my body: lots of vegetables, plenty of water, and some vitamin supplements. I developed a great breakfast, which I heartily recommend for everyone. It provides a lot of nutrients, has a low glycemic index, lowers cholesterol, stabilizes blood sugar, is full of fiber, and assists weight loss. On our western diet our blood pH tends to be low—i.e., too acidic. Anyone with a health problem usually has a much higher acidity because disease thrives in an acid environment. The first drink I have when I awake is a glass of water with lemon juice as this helps to neutralize the acid.

My Super Breakfast

1 part barley bran

1 part sesame seeds

1 part lecithin

Combine the above ingredients in a container, then keep in the fridge.

Boil 3 or 4 tablespoons of rolled oats. Pour the boiled oats into a bowl (great fiber—good for lowering blood pressure and blood sugar). Sprinkle a good serving of cinnamon (great for lowering blood sugar) onto the oats then add 2 heaped tablespoons of the above mixed ingredients into the bowl of oats with cinnamon. Mix, eat, and enjoy!

During the day I balanced my diet. I included bitter melon, which helps to lower blood pressure and blood sugar. I also drank a glass of water every waking hour as it also helps reduce blood pressure.

WARNING!

On no account should you stop using your medication without your doctor's prior approval.

Next I included regular exercise. I started walking (which was hard for me as my balance was gone). My first walk caused me a lot of fear and panic. I walked to the corner of my street—all of about 15 meters! I swayed like a drunk, but persisted. After a week I was able to walk around the block and my confidence increased. One excellent form of exercise that I started to do again was the Qigong walk for half an hour a day. I started using EMT on myself daily, which released the effect of many negative incidents in my life, including physical pain. I also lifted light weights three or four times a week and prayed and meditated daily for at least an hour. My sleeping started to improve and my balance became better after only three weeks.

However, I was still quite fragile. I worked on any negative thoughts by reprogramming my mind. If a negative thought crossed my mind, I would say (sometimes out loud) "DELETE!" and immediately filled my mind with pleasant thoughts. This process produced pleasant feelings. At night before I went to sleep I prayed, forgiving all the people and events in my life that hurt me, especially myself. It was a matter of releasing all feelings of guilt. Throughout the day I regularly expressed gratitude for all that I had: my family, my friends, and the healing that was taking place. This positive attitude and expectancy made me feel that my life was only getting better. I had developed a loving heart and no longer judged people or was critical of others as well as myself.

Apart from nutrition and exercise, the major component in my healing and in changing my attitude was correcting all the imbalances that interfered with the energy systems in my body and mind. Negative emotions can and do get trapped in different parts of the body, whether on a macro or a cellular level. No matter how many times you repeat a positive affirmation, it will have little influence unless the negative emotions are "unblocked," allowing energy to flow freely. It is then that the "magic" starts to happen.

EMT to the Rescue

By diligently going through the EMT procedure I found that I was able to enjoy the present moment. Previously, the past haunted and worried me and the future brought up fears. The present was nonexistent, yet it is the present that gives you the most power. If anything can be changed, it's the present. When I think of the past or the future, I think of it as being in the present moment—right NOW. It is here that you can mold your life and destiny. It took about six weeks before I started to feel my beautiful self again. I loved it! In a nutshell, I overcame my depression and felt joy, well-being (and, at times, euphoria) together with a gigantic leap in both emotional and physical strength, by doing the following on a daily basis:

1. Prayer and meditation

2. Proper nutrition

3. Exercise

4. EMT (energy therapy is the key that unlocks the place of all possibilities)

The support of my family and friends was invaluable. I now find it awe-inspiring to be able to help others with emotional afflictions and pain so they can reach a place of healing and feel life is worth living. It can be blissful once you release those heavy black holes.

They Have It In For You

When you are confronted with the onset of darkness that depression brings—act immediately! Prevention is by far better and easier to cure. Do your very best not to fall into the habit of the "poor me" attitude. Why? Because you will open up a whole Pandora's Box of negative emotions. At this stage you are very susceptible—it's like you have an open wound and got it infected.

My personal experiences were typical of the depressive state. One of the first signs I experienced while the darkness was shadowing my mind was confusion and the poor me attitude. My mind then started to try defending itself to prevent an onslaught. One way it did this was to slow or shut down almost completely its analytical thinking capacity.

I found it woefully hard to make decisions because now I was also preoccupied with trying to figure out what was going on within myself. I found myself relying more and more on other people to make decisions for me. That way, if anything went wrong, I would have somebody else to blame. At this stage I was in denial and convinced that everybody was wrong and I was the only one that is right.

When conversing with people, their words were just that, words, they had no meaning. A sentence meant nothing. They might as well have spoken in another language. The only time words made sense to me was when I gave them my own meaning. This in many cases was quite distorted, and no doubt one of the reasons it's so difficult to initially treat depression.

It's to your great advantage to be able to recognize telltale signs of depression because it's easier to treat and prevent depression when it's only in its infancy. Read on for more signals that you must be aware of. Please note that these do not always signify a disposition to depression.

However, it is better to be safe than sorry. Watch out for the following: when you find yourself *constantly* feeling agitated, perhaps when driving your car, where traffic lights annoy you and you are totally convinced that all other drivers on the road are wrong. And of course they are all there specifically to annoy you.

You also become easily offended and arguments occur in almost all conversations. If someone is explaining something to you, no matter what he or she is saying, you are 100% right. You completely ignore what the other person is saying and only have your own agenda as to what you are going to tell that person; in many cases it is something not even related to the discussion.

Things that did not annoy you before start to become intolerable—for example, people eating loudly or sneezing, they clothes they wear, and other personal traits may become offensive to you. I remember getting into heated arguments over the most trivial things. Logic was only a senseless word with no meaning whatsoever to me.

Once my wife complained that I did not put any sugar and stir her cup of coffee that I had made for her. Well, I just went berserk; I screamed and ranted how she dare even think I would do such a thing. You see, as far as I was concerned, I was perfect and never made mistakes. Fuming with anger, I stormed out the house and went straight to the pub.

While having a beer and at the same time beside myself with anger, one of my mates noticed I was upset and asked me what the problem was. When I told him about the coffee incident with my wife, he just looked at me in bewilderment and started to laugh. Seeing that I was not amused at his response, he abruptly stopped laughing. I immediately sensed that he thought I was going "nuts." I accused him of being very insensitive and not understanding at all.

His response was, Why bother about such a trivial incident? Boy, did this get me hot under the collar. Red faced, I shouted that it was the principle that was at stake here, and if I did not stand up to this onslaught all other "meanings" would collapse.

You see, I became very self-righteous and my arrogance showed itself in my speech as well as in my actions. Unknowingly at the time, I was tormenting myself with sheer trivia.

I sure was alienating a lot of my friends, but my poor family had no choice but to put up with my antics. There were times that they literally could not watch television while I was in the same room with them. I would just complain and yell at the shows that infringed on my newfound morality—in fact, all shows. News time was the worst.

I became judge and jury who wished all offenders, no matter how minor their offense or whoever differed from my opinions—to be executed or at least severely punished. Did it make sense to me? At the time it did.

If I was watching a comedy, no matter how funny it was I just could not laugh. All humor had gone. One of the beliefs that I took on was that if I laughed, I would have to pay for it. Something bad would happen to me. So feeling good had to stop immediately. Which reminds me, when I was about 6 years of age, my mother warned me that if I laughed that indeed something bad would happen.

That is a very good ingredient for depression, isn't it? She didn't know any better, bless her soul; her folks instilled this idea into her as well.

Anger is a relative of depression. With anger you still have the energy to express the emotion, even though at times you may wonder why you get so worked up over unrelated events. Some consider this just nervous energy. When your energy gets so depleted due to anger and you feel you are trapped, you begin to experience chronic hopelessness. You then start to have passive anger, because you are running on empty. Depressive symptoms start to surface.

A one-time business associate of mine, let's call him Roger, to conceal his true identity, decided he would become involved with my export business that I built from scratch. It was a product I developed and in which I put a lot of money—in all, $200,000, to be exact. Malaysia was my niche market.

Roger assured me he had great contacts in other Southeastern Asian countries, and that with his influence and help, my export business would expand significantly. Having known him for approximately 20 years, I took him at his word. We both traveled to different countries in this region, making contacts and forming concrete deals with companies that Roger had introduced me to. This went on for a period of three years. Eventually, these various contacts placed orders for my product, reassuring me that I would receive immediate payment into my bank account.

At this point I will spare you all the details. It so happened that the people we were meeting were his friends and I had been set up. They did not send me the money. As a result, I lost a substantial amount of money, while Roger and his cohorts made plenty. This almost made me bankrupt. The anger I had for these undesirables bordered on profound hatred, an emotion I never truly experienced. For Roger specifically, I felt sheer disbelief, disgust, and anger, with strong feelings of revenge.

After about three weeks, symptoms of depression became apparent. How many times must I live through these emotional torments, I thought to myself? No sleep and drinking to excess was the order of the day. My thoughts became suicidal; my animosity towards Roger grew larger every day. I had to act. I decided that I would drive interstate (for he lived in Sydney and I lived in Melbourne) and physically do him harm.

Mulling over these thoughts and the condition I was in scared me. I became paranoid. My attitude was one of deep mistrust for everybody. They all had it in for me. Do you think that it was only *my* fault that I was going through this unpleasantness? I will tell you now: Yes, it was. My attitude stunk. I let my emotions dictate my thoughts. Eventually, when I regained some sanity, I put off and did not harm Roger in any way.

Chapter 7

Choose Your Emotions or
They Will Choose You

◆

Our common experience is that we have a thought first, which is then followed by an emotion. Thoughts are energy just as the sun or gravity; they follow the laws of nature and the universe.

Thoughts also compel the mind to seek an appropriate emotion to give it a feeling, and at the same time strive to make some kind of sense that you are comfortable with. The mind communicates via words and pictures through all five senses.

What you picture in your mind and how clear you make it determines the intensity of your emotions and feelings. So the clearer and more intense the image, the quicker and more precise will be your response. In many cases, it only takes a fraction of a second. Your whole mood can and does change in a split second.

When your mood changes, the sequence of events perpetuates. You may have experienced this when you felt "stuck" with a particular emotion, much like when you get a song into your head and you just can't stop singing it in your mind or even at times out aloud.

If your thoughts produced it, then it's your thoughts that can change it. What I teach in my course is a very simple technique. All you do is take three deep breaths and then think of something totally different. Scramble the mind with other images. I suggest you produce four to five different themes in quick succession. Then when one of these pictures gives you that pleasant "buzz," you concentrate on that image for a short while. Two to three minutes is ample.

When the thought pattern is broken and the undesired thought is released, you will then feel a sense of calmness and peace. This is great to use especially when those small anomalies "pop up" during the day.

The problem arises when you start to feel negative emotions, without seemingly having negative thoughts preceding them. You seem to be driving in automatic negative emotions.

Your brain stores information deep in your subconscious mind—it's like a file system in a computer. The difference is that, with your computer, you need to press keys to retrieve information. Your subconscious mind has the uncanny ability to bring to your conscious mind past events, patterns, and memories without seemingly being consciously activated by you.

What You Feel You Will Find

Len was a very pleasant man in his early fifties. Ever since he was very young, Len's only concern was to enjoy himself. Nothing else mattered. He dropped out of school not because of he lacked academic prowess, but because he had an aversion to do any work. He had many jobs, none of which seemed to suit him. One of the slogans that he always repeated to himself was, "I just want freedom." He also repeated, "I don't want to be tied down to anything."

He proudly considered himself a "freedom fighter"—hence his going from job to job. In addition, when he pursued any course of study, he never completed it. And when he finally married, it only lasted ten years, which was a long commitment for Len.

It was at this stage that Len started to feel the symptoms of the dreaded depression. Being out of work, having very little money, and just recently divorced, Len was forced to reflect on his life. He saw his life as empty with little accomplishments. He had a lot of "If's." Len then went through a period where he blamed others and events in his life for his present condition. On his initial visit with me, I found him to be quite puzzling.

He had an optimistic personality. I found out later this was just a front that Len presented to others. Together, we also found, and to Len's surprise, that his thoughts did not match what was going on in his life. His thoughts did one thing and his actions did something else. Synchronization was missing. Self-rebellion was very evident. This was the key to his problem.

When Len was young he always had to work and help his father in business. He was constantly brainwashed into what career he must pursue. This affected him deeply, because he had to adapt to things he despised. He felt he was totally controlled. Not surprisingly, he rebelled as a teenager.

Len decided to do the Mindeze mentoring program, Misery to Bliss. He liked the idea that he could do this at home in his own time. What attracted him most was that he did not have any one peering into his life. And if he had any questions, he was able to contact Mindeze. Knowing Len's past records on completing courses, I had him make a commitment to me—that he must contact me weekly. He agreed.

As Len went through the questionnaire, he was able to pinpoint his problems one by one. The recognition of his faulty attitudes and negative emotions that did not serve him and the process of releasing these, instilled power into Len. For the first time he had experienced authentic self-control, which he relished.

First, he brought his pain and negative emotions down to alpha, which is an arbitrary intensity of zero. In the Misery to Bliss course (in both the home study course and the live workshops), I get the participants to measure the emotional intensity of they want to release. This is based on their own perception what they think the number would be for them. Intensity goes from 0 to 10, where 0 means the emotion or pain is nonexistent and 10 being the maximum.

For Len, the zero intensity meant that he felt as if he was in a realm of neutrality. Len described the experience—as if a heavy load were taken off his shoulders and the fog in his mind was at last clearing. It's where that sigh of relief happens and life becomes worth living again. In Len's own words: "I came from a place where I thought I would just have to live with it [depression], to a state of enormous relief, which is in itself is worth the effort."

Next, he chose the emotions that would serve him, followed by the thoughts, images, and self-talk that would trigger these desired emotions. Len found this part of the program exhilarating. He told me it was like going to a supermarket or a toy shop where he could pick and choose whatever he wanted to his heart's desire. At this stage he informed me that if he had possessed these skills earlier in life, he would have never had to go through all that pain. Len now had a desire to accomplish or at least finish some of the things he had started earlier in life. However, he was slightly apprehensive because of his age. I assured Len that it was never too late.

Just use your pass experiences, no matter how bad they were. And use them as a springboard to enter your life of bliss. (This is shown in the course.) Today, Len is in a business partnership and has never felt happier. It took Len approximately seven weeks form when he started the course to when he reached his desired results. His shift to a more positive attitude made it easier for him to change his life around for the better.

Adrian

Boy, if I ever heard more negative talk, including negative self-talk, Adrian would come close to taking first prize. If anything positive happened to him, it would quickly be overshadowed by his negativity. He always talked about the working class and how these people are constantly downtrodden. His ideal of utopia was that everybody was equal and that all should share their money around.

Adrian would ignore facts if they did not suit his philosophies. He complained about all levels of governments, all institutions, all rich people. His lifestyle reflected his attitude. Adrian was a highly strung individual with miserly qualities. When his pensioner parents received Meals on Wheels form the local council, he would take some of the food to eat at work.

Although he was a man of 38 years of age, he always listened to his parents. They ran his life. The sad fact was that they literally treated him like a slave. If Adrian wanted to go somewhere or buy something, he had to get permission from his father first. They managed his money and they managed his life. His parents would always discourage him from forming any kind of relationship with the opposite sex.

Adrian would always mention how grateful he was towards his parents. They would always tell him that they brought him into the world, so now he must pay them back. Adrian would take things literally. He never lied. I don't think he knew how. Unfortunately, some people would take advantage of him. Whenever this happened to him, he would experience extreme stress and anxiety. This would virtually cause him to lose all concepts of reality, so Adrian just couldn't cope. He would go into a fantasy world and deny that any such event had taken place. Adrian's world fell apart when his father died, with his mother then dying within a week.

Adrian fell into a deep depression. That's when he came to see me and told me his story. My first response was to explain to him that he cannot control what happens to him or the events around him, but he can take control of his attitudes towards what happens to himself. This way he will master any changes that happen to himself, rather than let it master him.

So I set Adrian a challenge: For him to take control of his life and not let others dictate what he should do. He was extremely gullible; what anybody told him he would totally believe them. To become the master rather than the slave he had been since he could remember, Adrian studied physics at University and loved the subject. To convince him of the power of imagination, which he now needed to practice, I quoted Albert Einstein to him: "Your imagination is your preview of life's coming attractions." For Adrian, this was an eye opener. He became a most enthusiastic student of the art of visualization, and very competent in creating images and emotions that served him. All during this time he was doing the mentoring program Misery to Bliss.

This program suggests that you concentrate on what works for you, because we are all individuals. For Adrian, it was hypnosis with some tapping. There is a chapter on self-hypnosis at the end of this book.

Adrian has come through with flying colors. In fact, he is now happily married.

This case demonstrates that if you want something bad enough (that is, if you are hungry enough), and with the right techniques that don't heavily infringe on your schedule, miracles do happen.

Chapter 8

Are You Hungry Yet?

You might have experienced hunger at some time in your life. I don't mean the sort that you have just before lunch or dinner. I mean a gut-wrenching hunger brought on by not eating for some time. This can be compared to your deepest yearnings: hunger for peace, financial stability, relationships, or an accomplishment; it can be absolutely anything that produces that deep, almost painful desiring.

I personally found that that during my depression, it was only when I had a deep desire to release my depression that I was able to take on the healing journey.

Medication, although it served its purpose, tended to make me procrastinate. I felt a "kind of relaxed feeling," so why bother doing anything. It was during these times that I started feeding my mind with positive thoughts and images. In actual fact, it became more important than eating food. For me, I must admit that the medication in my early stages of depression helped me to relax and meditate. This can be compared to getting a tow truck to bring your car to a repair shop if it had broken down. At the repair shop, your car gets fixed. For me, medication was the tow truck. The shop was my healing journey and getting off medication.

A sound mind brings everything into balance, and it's that which I wanted to reclaim.

As mentioned earlier, usually when you are in a state of depression, you feel that everybody is wrong and that you are the only one that is right. You believe no one understands you. In most cases, you are right. How do you come to the realization that you must do something about your state of mind? First, get your ego out the way and then, just for a few moments, pretending at first if you have to, think that what others are saying about you is right. A revelation will suddenly hit you: "Oh my gosh! Some of that stuff my friends and family were saying about me is true!" When you get this kind of thought—bingo! You have finally realized and accepted your disposition.

It is at this point that you will start to get that deep desire to become "normal," to return to the life of the living. You will do absolutely almost anything to get better. You are now halfway to gaining your emotional health back. Here is another relevant story.

Ann

According to Ann, she felt very comfortable; however, she did not fully realize that she was in a drugged stupor most of the day. If something upset her, she just popped another pill, which further sent her into a deeper stupor. It soon got to a stage that pills could not give her that relaxed feeling. So she began to drink wine every day, first a bottle then several bottles; a day did not pass without her drinking alcohol.

It got to the point that everything annoyed her. A fly would only have to land on her, or it would be windy outside, or the phone would ring, or someone asked her a question, and so on. On many occasions she had to get her neighbor to pick up her children from school because she was too drugged and drunk. Later Ann told me that life was like a haze during this period of her life. She found it increasingly difficult to distinguish between her dreams and waking life.

At times when Ann forgot to take her medication and reality started to creep in, she would virtually freak out, then unwisely double or even triple her dosage. The cycle would then start again. So what made her seek help?

It began to dawn on her: that ache was the feeling of life was fast passing her by plus all the goodies that could have made her life so much better and enjoyable. "God-given talents wasted on useless 'negativity' blocked by drugs and alcohol," Ann used to tell me on many occasions.

Ann was a very creative and excellent cook. Whenever Ann prepared a dish, in fact, her guests would always comment on how tasty and creative her dishes were. She was at home making main meals as she was whipping up desserts. Her cooking was always balanced. Unfortunately, her life was not so balanced.

Ann was only 34 years of age, yet she had a great fear of getting old. She would constantly look into the mirror and check for any wrinkles or grey hair. If she found an additional signs of age, she would get depressed—pills again. What Ann was not realizing was that she was actually living her "old age" in the present, instead of living her present age.

She informed me that it all started about ten years ago, when her husband seemed to lose interest in her. He kept commenting how on how beautiful she looked when she was younger. Ann tried everything to live up to his expectations. Beauty products galore, different hairdos with different colorings every month, diet, and that physically exhausting gym to stay in shape, all to no avail. In fact, her husband would ridicule her even more for her "failed" efforts. Not good for self-esteem, is it? It's about this time that Ann began to have superstitions that her husband was having an affair. As she recalls, it was also when her emotional problems had started.

Due to a lack of self-confidence, constant negative thoughts, and the pressure to look young and beautiful, it was not long before she began to suffer depression. Taking medication was the only way she could cope. Ann further compounded her situation by regularly and deliberately overdosing and of course drinking.

As already mentioned, when she finally reflected on her life, she did not like what she saw—a wasted life. It was at this stage that Ann had a burning desire to change. She felt she was lied to and got angry on many occasions for letting her be "sucked" in by her husband's negative comments about her.

She was now hungry to "fix herself up."

When she saw me, her main concern was to get off her medication as soon as possible. I put her on vitamin supplements because her body lacked the nutrition that would help her cope with withdrawal symptoms: Vitamins B and C, fish oil capsules, and magnesium. Later I included potassium. I also taught her the Qigong walk (Qigong is similar to Tai Chi). You can get information on Qigong at www.mindeze.com.

She purchased the ebook, *Free Your Spirit Heal Your Life*, before she started the program. This book contains information on how healing takes place, from a quantum physics perspective, some case histories, and some points on changing your attitude. This book can be found on the Mindeze site or at www.free-your-spirit-heal-your-life.com.

To instill and maintain her motivation and hunger for change, I had her reflect on the pain she experienced while being depressed and the anxiety it caused her. Then she had to think about the consequences if she decided to do nothing about her present condition: more pain and probably worse. According to Ann, this created a significant enough fear in her to stay wanting to change for the better. I then suggested that she chose some positive attributes she wanted to possess, and then create scenes where she was using these in real-life situations. She had to keep running these images as if she were watching a movie. She was to follow this procedure 5 times a day, more if negative thoughts started to creep up on her.

At times releasing some of her negative emotions was challenging. It was not until she was able to release her bitterness towards her husband that any real progress became evident. When she forgave herself for past mistakes and acquired a healthy love for herself, she progressed in leaps and bounds.

I can now report to you that after nine weeks, using my methods, Ann has reached her bliss. Unfortunately, there are a lot of Ann's out there. But the great news is that there is help from Misery to Bliss.

John

Unlike Ann, John found his bliss in recreational drugs. John's life seemed to be in real mess. He came from a well-to-do background; outwardly he lacked nothing in regard to material needs. John went to the best schools, and always had the best and latest gizmos. On his 18th birthday, he got a sports car from his parents. Anyone else would have been over the moon, but not John; he complained about the color. He sulked all day. Being a showoff, he just wanted to drive around and brag how good he was.

He equated being good with how many "things" someone possessed. This would irritate his friends. The first thing he would talk about when he met someone for the first time was about himself and how much he had. John did this to feel superior; he loved to see their reactions, and often referred them as "low lifes." I suppose you could characterize him as a "selfish brat." He always expected to get what he wanted, and when he went out with his friends, he had to be the center of attention, much to the annoyance of those around him.

When John completed his law degree, he was given a position in his father's law firm. For the first time he had to deal with people who did not share similar views with him, especially about himself. John felt it very difficult to be given orders, let alone follow them. He also lacked social communication skills, which resulted in his colleagues avoiding him. It was not until clients began requesting another attorney to work on their case that John started to feel like an outcast.

He soon realized that his so-called friends only stayed with him for one reason only; he paid for everything when they all went out. John's belief was that money can buy you everything. Some of John's friends knew about my work, and recommended that he see me. In retrospect, his friends hopped that I would change him into being a more tolerable human being.

On his first visit, I noticed that he displayed some of the classic symptoms of depression. He found it hard to sleep at night, had a poor appetite, had anxious thoughts, and started to develop a phobia—fear of crowds.

Whatever I suggested to John, he would always contradict me. On many occasions he would laugh openly, adding to my frustration to help him. His solution was a pill to help him sleep, a beer to increase his appetite, and to have nothing to do with those lowlife that he needed to deal with.

I suppose it was at this stage I felt that I did not want to work with him. It was a waste of time for him as well as for me. He did not need my services; he was not hungry enough to change. He just seemed to have a desire for self-gratification with no respect for others. He also gave a strong impression that he knew everything—he had all the answers—and had everything he needed and wanted. The only noticeable thing he did not have was peace of mind.

It was no use talking to him about changing his attitude. His self-reliance closed off all forms of communication, especially in this area, even when I told him that trying to find peace of mind with his present attitude would only make things worse and more complicated if he did not address this important issue. He just laughed, mockingly, and told me that he could easily go around me and buy this "peace of mind." In a strange way, I felt sorry for him because I could almost predict with certainty where he would be at in the next three years. We parted amiably, wishing each other the best.

It was almost two years later that I heard John was drinking heavily and taking drugs. He was in a hellhole, a place where he let his negative thoughts, attitudes, and emotions take his mind to. The place of torment stuck in his misery, consciously and unconsciously refusing his rightful place of bliss.

Do I worry about such people? Of course I do. It actually frustrates me to no end that they are not hungry enough to change, especially when there are tools like Misery to Bliss to guide them back to emotional health and well-being. Why travel second or third class in your life's journey when you can go first class? John, if by chance you are reading this book (I am sure you recognize it's you in this story), please, I urge you contact me and let's start all over again.

Chapter 9

Fog Everywhere—Learning

---◆---

I just had to add this chapter; it's a very important topic that cannot be ignored. Being both a student and teacher has brought to my attention a most important and urgent need to help all learners—whether you are at junior or secondary school at university—in fact, anyone who learns—and that's most of us. This is for you.

As a human being, you are constantly learning, from the time you come on to this planet until the time you leave it. The very foundation of your life is based on learning. You cannot escape it. Civilizations advance because of learning; it is one of the criteria for your existence. Your skills at how you learn ultimately dictate your lifestyle to a large extent. Your capability to learn opens a myriad of opportunities. It can make life exciting. There is absolutely not one thing that has not been the result of learning.

My emphasis is on educating any student who wants to make learning as easy as breathing and eating. Also, anyone who has learning problems, such as difficulty in understanding what they have just read. Comprehension is a big problem, so is being able to deduce, add, subtract, compute, remember, and that terror—exam jitters. If learning causes you stress, anxiety, depression, or other negative emotions that are out of your control, then this is a must program for you.

There are three ways of learning: visual, kinesthetic, or auditory. You may use one or a combination of these means to learn; no matter which way you learn, you are always using your emotions. Therefore, having healthy and balanced emotions are the most important component to learning.

You react to what you read, hear, or see via your emotions, which are connected to your thoughts and your nervous system. Emotional health and well-being are essential to your learning processes.

When you have negative emotions and feelings released, you are then emotionally balanced; you will get the maximum benefits, especially with the ease of learning you will experience. As mentioned, negative emotions distort your nervous system, which at the best of times makes learning very difficult. It also confuses your decision making to no end. So the first thing you need to do is to release all negative emotions that are deeply embedded in your subconscious. This will clear the path for your thought processes to flow freely and unhindered. One of the great side effects of this is that you will be able to handle any negative emotions that you may be confronted with in the future. This will result in you being able to springboard into a more positive learning environment.

When your mind is relaxed and having fun, it will want to stay in that zone for longer periods.

Ah, what benefits! Your focus is greatly magnified, memory is highly awakened, reason and analytical skills are absolutely enhanced. Then a major reward is in store for you. That wonderful intuitive mind "kicks in." Now you have it, both left and right hemispheres of your brain working like a well-tuned machine, smoothly running effortlessly, serving all your learning needs.

Thomas

Thomas was a 14-year-old student who had problems with English and math. His mother told me that he studied hard almost every day, spending up to five hours at his desk. Unfortunately, his results certainly did not reflect his hard work. I personally do not recommend a 14-year-old to be studying these long hours. When Tom visited me, I had him read a passage from his book aloud. He found this exercise very difficult. I would say that he read like a 5-year-old. His math was no better.

Frustration was evident every time Thomas tried reading. By the way, if you are wondering, he also had the same problem when he read to himself. The more he tried the more tense he got—and the less he was able to cope. Tears would start to flow and in desperation he would just stop reading. How he was able to stay at school with his problem not addressed amazed me.

Then, again, the education system is geared to get the masses through rather than deal with individual who have difficulties. Sure, some schools have programs, and excellent ones at that. But the problem is that intervention to address learning problems that some students experience happens far too late. Another problem is that the established learning institutions on the whole fail to implement other methods than their own. Who misses out? The poor student.

Thomas was troubled with emotional issues that were the results of his teacher belittling him in front of the class and being bullied by some of his fellow students. He was a timid boy who was fair game to the more aggressive boys. His learning dysfunction, particularly in his case, dyslexia, resulted from emotional stress at the time of learning. The stress was probably so intense that his mind would virtually program a blind spot to a given learning skill due to fear. His negative emotions or feelings could have been associated with fear and pain of ridicule, or pain itself. His consequent failures would have been repeated time and again, each time compounding his whole negative experience with learning, and no doubt with being at school.

Thomas's belief system was based on emotional pain associated with learning. Stress, anxiety, and depression became a way of life for this poor boy. He would use all sorts of strategies in the hope of masking his shortcomings. One of his favorites was "I have a headache" and then request to go to sick bay; this was more prevalent when he had to sit for a test. School was miserable for him. Thomas once told me that the two things that he most dreaded was to be asked to read in front of the class, and the teacher calling out his low marks in front of everybody in the classroom. This caused him enormous embarrassment. Is it any wonder Thomas had trouble sleeping and a poor appetite?

Every session, one of the first things I would get Thomas to do was to get him to "cross crawl." I would get him to march in one spot, lifting his knees up high; at the same time, he had to cross one hand over and touch the opposite knee while the knee was in the high lifted position, and then do the reverse with the other hand and knee. He would repeat this for about three minutes.

At the same time he would sing out numbers: 1–2–3–4–etc. This is one way to integrate both hemispheres of the brain. Balance is achieved when both sides of the brain can easily and freely communicate with each other. Cross crawls are good to do when you have been using one side of the brain more than the other.

It's all about balance. Through scientific research, it is now commonly accepted that the left and right sides of the brain have different functions. Overlapping frequently occurs.

LEFT SIDE:	RIGHT SIDE:
Linear	Creative
Specific focus	Focused on the whole
Survival	Unlimited perception
Analytical	Spatial
Time oriented	No time limitation
Verbal language	Language: image/color
Self-image	Symbols
Judgmental	Rhythmic/musical
Belief system	Nonjudgmental

Another way to balance your left and right hemispheres is to simply sing or hum a tune, then count to 10, and repeat this 3 or 5 times. I won't force you to sing hearing how you sing, just hum then.

Stimulating your brain is essential because it extends out and controls your entire nervous system. The brain, as do the nerve synapses (a synapse is the region of contact between the processes of two or more nerve cells across which an impulse passes), function on an all-or-nothing basis. If the stimulus is not high enough (due to a blockage produced either by a physical or by an emotional dysfunction) for a particular nerve cell, you will not get a response. It's much the same way as heating water to reach 100°C so it can boil; any temperature below that and the water will not boil.

Releasing Thomas's negative emotions and accentuating the positive encouraged Thomas considerably. He faithfully followed the program and in approximately three weeks Tom was reading and studying with ease much to the delight of his mother. His emotions also stabilized. You or your loved ones can also get the same results. Look for the program Mindeze Gym at mindezegym.com.

Chapter 10

Good News—WOW!

Do you want the bad news or the good news first? Let me guess! Yes, you want the bad news first. OK. The bad news is that if you do nothing about your problem, it will get worse. It doesn't take a rocket scientist to figure that one out. Just let me clarify this one, though. Yes, it could happen that you come out of your depression if you don't attend to it. The drawback is that it takes an awfully long time. Sometimes years of suffering has to be endured before any relief is felt. The pitfall here is that you can go back into depression very quickly. Why? You have not resolved or released any of the issues that caused it to appear in the first place: you have subconscious memories of what triggered the depression. Well, guess what? All you need is just a smidgen of recall about a situation or event that your memory recognizes as depression (remember, it is still wired in your brain)—and bang!—"here you go again." Not very pleasant, especially when you thought it was all over.

That being said, it just makes sense to confront and fix the problem as soon as you recognize that its ugly head had risen. The good news is, then, that you CAN fix it. And fix it you will, without a doubt. If others can, so can you.

You have to know you have a problem to be able to fix it. I assume that you have read the chapter, "Know the Mind of Your Enemy." After you have conceded you have a problem, the first thing you need to do is to write down either on paper or on your computer all the negative feelings and other experiences that you are having. Why? As Glenn Dietzel in his course, "Awaken the Author Within," states, "Writing is the doing part of thinking." You actually awaken your subconscious mind when you write, and you will be surprised how much is revealed to you by doing this simple exercise. Please don't worry if you write about stuff that does not make sense to you. This always happens when you first start to write.

Remember, there is a lot of turmoil going on in your mind, and what you are doing is bringing out into the open just what is going on in your mind.

You will discover new things about yourself, such as weaknesses but especially strengths you never thought you had before. Writing will also give you hints how to win the battles of your depression and, more importantly, finally conquering it. As Francis Bacon once said, "Write down the thoughts of the moment. Those that come unsought for are commonly the most valuable."

Never ever underestimate the power of writing. You will find it's a quick way to healing. You must learn to relax in every situation. How? Don't take yourself seriously; know that you are part of the human race and interconnected with the universe. You are a player that has a purpose in creation. Believe it or not, what you are going through is meant to be. This may seem a cruel statement, but the reason why you are experiencing this torment is that a strength that you have is trying to reveal itself to you; however, your fears and doubts have prevented you from claiming what is rightfully yours. You just can't keep pretending and pushing away what needs to be acknowledged and attended to. Keep this in mind and maintain an unshakable faith with absolutely no doubt that you will eliminate depression and its allies, negative emotions. You will thus be in a position to go for it.

One quick and effective way to release unwanted negative thoughts or emotions that you can do any time, even while driving a car, is to do some self-talk. For example, if you happen to be experiencing anxiety followed by depression when you have to visit some friends, you can say to yourself, first:

"Sure I have this anxiety that causes me depression; I don't know where it comes from or why it causes me so much anguish. I will just accept for what it is, a pain in the butt. I certainly will not analyze it, for the feelings defy all logic; therefore, it would be a waste of time and effort to try to work it out. So *stuff* the why's and how's of this anxiety."

Second, say,

"I will make this anxiety my best friend, a person I know I can talk to, who will understand me. This anxiety at the moment is part of me. There is no denying that. So now my friend, anxiety, you came from somewhere. I thank you for your visit. I don't really need you now, so go back to where you came from. By the way, I am going to release you."

Third, say, "When do I want to release anxiety? I chose now to release you. Go then."

Then take 3 deep breaths, and with each outbreath say, "Anxiety gone, relax."

You are self-talking directly to your subconscious—let it go and release—putting yourself in charge of your life.

If you want something, you are actually telling your subconscious you lack it, so it gives you more lack. Fears, worries, and concerns are the root of all your problems. If you let go of wanting:

- control

- approval

- safety/security

you will get to the place of "having" when you rid yourself of all your negative feelings and emotions.

Don't ignore, suppress, express, or run away from your negative issues. Admit that you have them and that you are responsible for their presence. Don't try to analyze how they are released—this is strictly experiential. You will start feeling better and better as you let go. Letting go of your negatives will only allow room for positives and it's then that good things start to happen for you. In this frame of mind, the "allowing release" can happen and you gain benefits. Here is another effective technique:

1. Bring the feeling into your awareness. Feel it. Give it an intensity 0 to 10 (0 indicates the negative feeling is all gone and 10 indicates the negative is most intense). It can be a present, past, or a preconceived future issue.

2. Could I just let it go? (If no, tap your "magic button"? which is a point on the body, predominately in the head, chest, or stomach area, that is associated with an acupuncture point that you can find by using mus-

cle testing, as in kinesiology?until you can say yes, as shown in the Misery to Bliss home course.) Or hold your forehead with one hand. Relax until you feel you can say yes.

3. When you get to yes, ask yourself, Do I want to let it go? (Use the magic button if necessary, until you get a yes.) Or hold your forehead as in Step 2.

4. When can I let this go? Say NOW.

5. Let go and release.

Here is how to perform Step 5:

When letting go and releasing, imagine an opening in your stomach, chest, and forehead area. These openings reach deep down into these areas via large vents. Now imagine that the negative feeling (it can be in the form of dark smoke or water—remember its only energy) starts to flow out of these areas. It's only the feeling you focus on—not the issue. For example, if you have that butterfly feeling in your stomach, it's that feeling you would concentrate on, not why and how it got there. You just keep bringing it up into your awareness and let go as I have explained until the feeling is all gone. It now has a "0" intensity.

Always let go and release negative emotions. You can do this anytime, anywhere whenever you get that negative feeling. The beauty about this is that you can let go and release in front of people, and they won't have a clue that you are in fact letting go of your negative feelings right in front of them.

I suggest you go back as far as you can remember and release all those negative feelings.

Anxiety, depression, stress, fears, anger, phobias-look in the booklet that comes with the Misery to Bliss home study course and workshops. You can also refer to the negative emotions listed in Chapter 4.

Now allow yourself to "have." The sayings must be in the positive and in the present (see Chapter 13 for a further explanation of positive and present tense statements). Here are some examples:

"I allow myself to have emotional well-being with ease."

"I allow myself to have the perfect relationship with ease."

"I allow myself to let go of all my negative feelings with ease."

"I allow myself to have financial abundance with ease."

I can assure you if you follow the procedures on a regular basis, preferably daily, you will definitely get positive results. When you release the negative feelings, you only have positive feelings to take their place. With these positive feelings, positive things start to happen in your life. Now it's all up to you to practice until it becomes second nature. I can assure you that you will find your bliss.

Chapter 11

Geometry of Conquering Depression

◆

The Jagged Circle With Internal Chaotic Waves

This represents a state of turmoil and confusion. The jaggedness shows how your depression does not quite fit into your surroundings and at the same time you try to hide from people. You don't see any hope, yet somehow hang in there. You know that if the circle and its internal chaos unravel, you feel you will be lost forever.

At least in an irregular way you seem to be coping. Steering your mind to do what you want it to do is a constant struggle. You always feel you are off course, but come back to the circle, where you experience moments of sanity. This is where you don't quite know your destination, like being on a roller coaster hurtling out of control. At any given moment it can go off the rails. It's the real fear of waiting for madness to finally devour you. Even onlookers sense and smell your fear—hence, they avoid you. A feeling of loneliness and helplessness that no one understands your predicament becomes stronger than ever. You feel like a freak.

The chaotic waves indicate no direction; you feel you have no control over your innermost thoughts. Here wrong judgments and decisions are made. This is where you are mainly focused—producing yet again more turmoil. No inner peace can ever be experienced here.

A Dot

One arrow will not hit 100 dots or bull's-eye. One arrow can only hit one dot. So what you focus on you will eventually get. If you focus on 100 different things, you have a very slim chance of getting what you want. It will be random. It will cause frustration. The one you get is the one that has been given the most attention to, whether it was at your conscious or subconscious level. Think of it like using a magnifying glass to set some paper on fire. By moving the magnifying glass here and there over the paper, you are scattering the potential energy of the sun. However, if you concentrate your magnifying glass on one spot, focusing all the energy of the sun there—Wow! the paper lights up—and quite quickly at that. Focus is the "magic" that will eventually produce results.

Suffice it to say that it's best if you set your focus on what you want rather than what you don't want. Whatever you choose will be manifested in your life. So if your desire is to beat depression, all your thought must be one of "I am healed" or "Every second, whether I am asleep or awake, healing is taking place within me" then again " I am grateful for this healing, my mind is clear." As soon as you start to feel the onset of depression or anxiety, go back to your focal point and go over these sayings, quietly to your self, or if no one is around, shout or sing it out with complete joy. By doing this, you are scrambling the negative thoughts that are coming into your mind. Don't give them a chance to fester in your mind. They will only give you false information and this is the last thing you need. Thus, as with the dot, focus only on the desired end result.

Vertical Line

If you want to get better, the only way is up; however, there is one important criterion you need to implement. If you are going to construct a tall building, guess what you need to do first, given you already have the blueprints? A strong foundation! Just like a large tree needs strong roots to anchor itself deep into the ground so it can stand upright, resist most of Mother Nature's onslaughts, and provide water and nutrients to all its branches and leaves. The tall building does much the same; it is also anchored, so it stands erect. Within its corridors and rooms, all sorts of activities take place.

There are wirings, pipes, escalators, lifts, elevators, etc., all able to be housed because of a strong foundation.

Now that you are focused, build this foundation. Here are a few ways you can do this:

- Meditation and self-hypnosis (I will give you a guided method in the bonus chapter at the end of this book).

- Eat plenty of vegetables and fruit. Avoid processed food. As I have mentioned already, some of the additives in these foods can trigger depression. In fact, some new research has shown this to be the case, especially with MSG (monosodium glutamate). Don't stress out; you don't have to totally avoid them. Once or twice a week is OK.

- Exercise. Try ½ hour a day. Just walking is excellent. Persistence is the key. I personally do the "Qigong Walk," which I also teach my clients, with excellent results. In fact, this activity alone has helped some participants feel 30% to 70% better. Some have reported that doing this exercise alone cleared their depression. I also teach this in my program.

- Drink plenty of water. I know I have said this before. A glass every hour is ideal.

It's all about reducing stress to a minimum, so you can use this energy to become a winner in your quest for emotional well-being.

By the way, I'm not talking about just survival here. I am setting you up to be the total conqueror of your depression and negative emotions. To do this, you collect the best armaments—correct foods, nutrients, and vitamins—to release toxins that pollute both your body and mind.

Choose the best weapons. These would include exercise, self-hypnosis, meditation, and of course EMT (this is presented in the course, Misery to Bliss).

Put it this way: you have been at the bottom of the pit; you can't descend any further and you're scrapping the bottom. The only direction for you to take now is up. Be joyful. You have focused on your target and now you have aligned the target with the line going straight up to obtain your desired outcome—and that is conquering depression! As you are aware, the shortest distance between 2 points is a straight line. That is why being in your misery then reaching your bliss is obtained a lot faster when you go straight for it, without trying to find out how it all works. I have already done that for you. Enjoy the process and celebrate the positive results. Your journey has begun.

What would be a great way to monitor your progress? Yes, write. This way you will have something tangible to look at, a way of measuring where you are and how far you have progressed.

Horizontal Line

This is the platform from which you will work. Travel "light" is always the best advice given by many fellow travelers. Why carry unnecessary garbage? Pack all your negative emotions away on the horizontal line, a platform that is very sturdy and strong. Put it away and only open it when you wish to see what you have learned and how you dealt with that particular negative emotion. It's great for future use.

Did you realize that you have been carrying these negative emotions as you would sacks of potatoes, weighing you down and expending unnecessary energy? Admittedly, some of you carry larger sacks than others. It doesn't matter; just gently put that heavy load down. The heavier the load, the greater the relief you will experience. Get rid of each negative emotion one by one. Generally, the more thorough you are, the better the results. How can you do this? Here is one method I have used.

Sit down in a quite place. Relax. Then go back as far as you can remember. Now choose a negative emotion connected to an event or situation that has upset you. Rate each one 0 to 10 (10 indicated the most intense and 0 indicating it is a nonissue). (More techniques can be found in the Misery to Bliss program.)

When you are fully relaxed, or at least as relaxed as you can possibly feel, do the following:

Put an image in your mind of the situation that you have chosen, a large picture, bright in color. Try to put all your senses into your image that caused the negative emotion. It could be fear, anxiety, or other negative feelings. Now put your open hand on your forehead and with the other open hand hold the back of your head. While doing this, hum, any tune will do; at the same time, look down to the left (eyes only—don't move your head) Then look down to the right. Next, move your eyes around one way the other way. Look side to side. After about 2 minutes, just close your eyes and relax, with your hands still wrapped around your head. Finally, tap the top of your head with 2 fingers, for about a minute. Put your arms down and sit quietly for about a minute. Then come up with an intensity number for that particular event you are releasing. If it is not 0, repeat the process until you go down to 0. Can't think of a number? Don't worry—just guess. Your guess will be right.

The most important part of all the exercises is **DON'T ANALYZE.** Just flow with it. It's the negative feelings that have no logical explanation that are what you want to release. Let it happen.

Please be patient with yourself. You don't have to complete everything in one sitting. It's your choice how much you want to do in one sitting. Another important aspect of the exercise is to forgive yourself, other people, and the particular events as best you can. You can do this at the beginning, in the middle, or at the end of your sitting. Also, after each release express gratitude and thankfulness to God, an angel, a saint, a friend, whoever is right for you. Relax and smile.

The Triangle

To remain in a state of well-being you need to attend to your physical, emotional, and spiritual needs.

This is the **Tricode** of life. All are important for balanced living. Human beings follow this tricode sequence from birth to death. When newly born and at infancy, the physical aspect of the code is the priority. Nutrition for body growth and nurturing is no doubt the most needed at this early stage. Into your teens and early adulthood, emotional growth takes precedence. Emotions are learned. You are beginning to define your personality.

As you get older and start to enter your golden years, spirituality becomes the main theme. Your readiness to take your ultimate journey is defined by your acceptance of all things in life, old and new.

Now imagine this triangle spinning around, sometimes slowly, at other times quickly. The Tricode is not static, but represents continuous change and growth. It demands it. Rebirth and regrowth forever strive to reach the pinnacle of your life's creation, as it is expressed through each unique individual.

Your devotion and willingness to learn, either through personal experiences or from others who have traveled the road before you, is your choice. Learning from the wise and learned will guide you to new horizons much quicker.

Stubbornness and arrogance do not have a place here. Love, acceptance, and harmony do. To a large extent, your depression is also the result of your unwillingness to change. Admittedly, change can be painful at times. But as I have experienced, it's better to have a painful change than put up with a dreadful depression. Then again, change does not always have to be painful.

When I knew I had to make a change for my overall benefit, I would imagine that I was preparing to travel abroad, for a relaxing holiday, to an exotic fascinating destination. If you don't like traveling, pick something else that is pleasant for you, that you can correlate with change. You will be surprised how easy and pleasant change can be. As I have already mentioned, acceptance is the first step in healing your depression. Don't worry about how far gone you think you are, or how old you are. Just start where you are at. Go at your own pace.

Choose a negative emotion from the Tricode of life—work on it until you are 100% satisfied. You can use colors to help yourself heal this negative emotion. Any color that comes to mind will do, although one's favorite colors seem to help. Then sit back and admire the colors of the spinning triangle. Watch in awe and feel the bliss.

The Circle

No beginning and no end—Just being—A place of bliss. Your intentions are extremely powerful; they actually form your thoughts, which in turn offset an emotion. If your intention is to get sick, you have a greater than normal possibility to get sick. It's also true for many other things in life. Poor intention creates poorly made results.

It is also here that relativity is apparent. If you place your finger on a hot stove for a second, that second will feel like an hour. Having a great time with your friend for an hour will only seem like a second. A fifty dollar note may mean a lot to a poor person; however, it could mean very little to a rich man.

Now imagine you are a tiny atom within the circle; relative to you, the road is straight. However, if for any reason you think it's not straight, you may make a turn and off the circle of bliss is the result. This happens to you with the onset of depression. For some reason you think, either consciously or unconsciously, you need to change direction. This is caused by fears and other negative emotions.

When you are in unfamiliar territory and traveling on roads you have never seen before, you become frustrated, angry, then fearful of the unknown. If you try to make decisions from this frame of mind, it's no wonder you will find it almost impossible to get back on track.

Meditative self-hypnosis is a great way to get back into the circle, an atmosphere of peace. Happy and contented thoughts are more easily produced in this state. A joyful soul sees adventure in everything. An attitude of trust, faith, belief in yourself and a higher power than you will help bring about emotional well-being. Depression will be a thing of the past.

In the thousands of people that I have helped with depression and other emotional ailments, I have found that people who had a belief in God or were spiritual tended to heal easier and faster. My suggestion, then, is if you have any kind of spiritual affiliation, embrace it. If you don't, seek and find one. As you may have probably already read or heard—you are a spirit first then a body, not the other way round. It thus makes good sense to attend to your spiritual needs.

A book that I have written that you may find helpful in this area is at www.free-your-spirit-heal-your-life.com. Check it out.

Here is a simple exercise that I call the "Circle of Excellence." It's something I learned while I was taking my course in natural healing. Its effectiveness has stood the test of time. I practice this myself and teach my clients how to do it as well. You can do this whenever you want to enhance and anchor any positive emotions.

Draw a circle on the ground, large enough for you to stand in. Then write down on paper what positive emotion you want to serve you. Say, for example, you want confidence. I am talking about confidence in general here, not confidence in a specific area. If you played some uplifting music, perhaps a song by your favorite singer, it would add to the effectiveness of the exercise. Let's begin. Now, project into the circle and onto yourself a time when you were absolutely confident. With the music playing, physically step into the circle. While standing in the circle of confidence, feel and imagine that you are completely absorbed with your whole being, with confidence. Dance, sing, and yell out that you are the most confident person in the world. Within this circle feel the frequency and vibration of confidence, if you can't visualize it. Come up with a color that represents your confidence; surround yourself with this color, breath it in, let it reach every living cell in your body. Absorb this calmness as your feeling of confidence excites and enraptures you.

Give thanks, and feel gratitude for your newfound confidence. Think of ways you can use it to your advantage.

How is it going to change your life? While still standing in the circle, clear all thoughts and relax; feel the calmness for about a minute, then step out of the circle. Your final step is to test your confidence. This is best done by getting yourself into a situation that requires you to have confidence to carry out a particular task. You will be pleasantly surprised at the result. And of course you can do The Circle of Excellence as many times as you like, for the same thing, and for any other positive emotion you want instilled into your subconscious to serve you. Some of my participants have also used this exercise to help them with physical healing, producing some great results.

At times it is the simplest things that will give you the best results. By the way, you can do The Circle of Excellence in your mind as well. How convenient would this be, for example, while you a flying in a plane or to prepare for that all-important meeting.

Chapter 12

Some Important Connections

---◆---

For emotional guidance, use your heart and a positive attitude to run your life. It has been recently discovered by molecular biologists that the heart is the body's most important endocrine gland. It responds to your experience of the world, producing and releasing a major hormone—ANF, which stands for atriol neuriatic factor—that profoundly effects every operation in the limbic structure. The limbic area is the emotional brain. It contains the hippocampus, where memory and learning take place, and the hypothalamus, which is the control center for the entire hormonal system. It is now known that 60 to 65% of the cells of the heart are actually neural cells, not muscle cells as previously believed, with the same neurotransmitters as the brain.

Quite literally, then, there is a "brain" in your heart linked to every major organ in your body and to the entire muscle spindle system that uniquely enables you to express all your emotions.

Thus, is a dialogue between the brain of the heart and the emotional brain 24 hours a day that we are not even aware of. The heart responds to messages sent to it from the emotional brain. The emotional brain makes a qualitative evaluation of your experiences in your surroundings and sends this information at every instant down to your heart. In return, the heart exhorts the brain to make the appropriate response. Of course, this all occurs at the nonverbal level.

What this means is that the responses that the heart makes affects the entire human system. Meanwhile, biophysicists have discovered that the heart is also a very powerful electromagnetic generator. It creates an electromagnetic field that encompasses the body and extends out anywhere from eight to twelve feet away from it. It is so powerful that you can take an electrocardiogram reading from as far as three feet away from the body. Is it any wonder that you can sense other people's emotional state? It won't be too long before we will be able to read people's minds as well. In fact, some people who are more sensitive to this kind of energy can do this already.

The field that your heart produces is holographic in nature, meaning that you can read it from any point on the body and from any point within the field. No matter how microscopic the sample is, you can receive the information of the entire field. What is intriguing is how profoundly this electromagnetic field affects the brain. All indications are that it furnishes the whole radio wave spectrum from which the brain draws its material to create your internal experience of the world.

Perhaps most importantly, it is known that the spectrum of

Richard Link

the heart is profoundly affected by your emotional response to your world. Your emotional response changes your heart's electromagnetic spectrum, which is what your brain feeds on. Ultimately, everything in your life hinges on your emotional response to specific events. We need to think more with our hearts, for therein lies the secret to our emotional well-being. Where do you start? With your intentions.

Higher intentions are more powerful than lower intentions. Therefore, intentions of a higher frequency will prevail over those of a lower frequency. So what you give more attention to in your mind with powerful emotions will result in your final outcome. If you are half-hearted about something, for example, conquering depression, you will get only half the result you want.

In my experience, and this holds true for many others in the natural health field, I have found that the organs in the human body, as you have already seen with the heart–brain connection, are all connected to and respond to your emotional states. Your positive thoughts will produce positive reactions in the particular organ associated with it.

The same is true for negative thoughts. For example, the emotion of fear will predominately affect your kidneys. Have you ever experienced real fear, then noticed you had a physical throbbing sensation in your kidney area? The emotion of worry affects your pancreas. My father ran a business, and I remember him constantly worrying; he always tried his best to suppress it at all costs. In the end, he certainly paid for it. He got pancreatic cancer and died from it. Other factors not doubt contributed to his condition, which I will not get into here. Suffice to say worry was one of the major contributors. Now please don't get all upset and worried. That was an example of an extreme case.

Emotional well-being is an attainable goal for everyone. You can view the correlation between your emotions and body organs as a way of communication—each knows what needs to be done to bring about balance. Depression has been and always will be conquered by many of its past sufferers.

Please enjoy the next bonus chapter, the lucky 13. It gives you some examples of the benefits of meditative hypnosis, and a practical guide of how to go about it. Read it over first to get an idea of the process. Then just do it. Some closing comments will also be given.

Chapter 13

A Practical Guide to
Meditative Hypnosis

There are many benefits you can receive from meditating on a regular basis. The first is to tame the wild mind from mood swings, moving between the past to the future with a clinging or aversion, spending little time in the present.

The second is to observe the thoughts and sensations in the body without an attachment to this clinging or aversion, as happens in depression. Just allowing is the key here. Meditation is observation of the inner self, to purify the mind.

Very few people give themselves time out each day for introspection; they tend to live a life of reacting to situation after situation and then wonder why they suffer so much. The layers of negative reactions multiply and pile up so high that even the smallest inconvenience can unleash a raging fury, or bring them to their knees in despair and depression. Their minds become unbalanced. With meditation and hypnosis, they can tame their minds.

Read the following instructions first, and then apply the techniques; it does not have to be word for word. You can come up with your own words.

Hypnosis Is Natural

The first thing you need to know is that hypnosis is a very natural state. It requires no special power to hypnotize someone. If you can talk, you can hypnotize.

In fact, it is such a natural state that people go into hypnosis regularly without even realizing it. The most common natural states occur while gazing into a fire or when driving (it's that moment when you suddenly realize that you are unsure by which route you have just driven home!). If you were to listen to some positive suggestions while in these naturally occurring trance states, they would have an effect on you…so be aware of commercial radio on long journeys!

When you intentionally hypnotize yourself, what you are doing is operating the switch that puts you into this natural state at a time of your choosing so that you can use it productively.

Relaxation Causes Trance

There are many things that have been found to cause a trance; these include confusion, shock, repetition, focused attention, and relaxation. Here you are going to be concentrating on relaxation, because it is the easiest to produce.

You will also be using focused attention; this will help to stop your mind from wandering during the induction process.

The initial induction process is all about getting yourself to relax. You probably have forgotten how to do this completely. I will help you out; most of you are a lot more tenser than you realize.

Relaxing

Before you actually begin the hypnotic process, it's a good idea to do a few physical relaxation exercises. This will put you in a much more responsive state during the actual induction and save you time.

The easiest and most effective way to do this is to tense and relax your muscles. Start with the face by screwing it up nice and tight, hold it for a few seconds, and then relax. Next, scrunch your shoulders, hold, then relax. Move on to arms, torso, stomach area, upper (then lower) legs, and finally feet. When tensing the legs and feet, be sure to pull your toes and feet up towards the body rather than pointing them out straight as this could cause cramp.

You should also be aware that if tensing a certain area might be unwise due to health problems, you can simply skip that area. For example, you might be suffering from a hernia.

Once you have systematically tensed and relaxed each area, then tense and relax the entire body in one go. This simple exercise will release a lot of tension and set you up nicely for the induction process.

Induction Process

Now that you know that relaxation and focused attention are two of the keys to successfully induce a hypnotic state, you are ready to learn the induction script. I have laid out a script for you word for word below, but these words are not some kind of mystical incantation, they are not a spell that produces trance, they are simply a suggestive list of instructions and commands that will produce a relaxed state. You can just as easily make up your own inducted script using this one as a guide. The goal is to get you to relax, so use your imagination and embellish on what I have given you here.

Use a basic monotone voice as you speak clearly and slowly to yourself. As the trance progresses, your voice should slow down so that you complement your relaxed state.

The Induction Script

Focus your gaze on an imaginary spot on the ceiling. Then count 1 to 10. When you say one (1), close your eyes. Even when your eyes are closed, keep focused on the imaginary spot on the ceiling. Ready? Close your eyes now, but keep them in position.

1. Now slowly open them.

2. Closing your eyes again, notice how comfortable it feels to let them rest.

3. Now slowly open them, continuing to gaze at the spot.

4. Closing down easily and slowly while you listen to your own voice.

5. Slowly open.

6. Closing down now and very soon your eyelids will begin to feel very tired and heavy.

7. Nice and slow.

8. Just letting them close down now, so comfortable, so heavy and relaxed.

9. Slowly open them and focus on that spot.

10. More and more heavy with each number now. That's fine. More and more relaxed as your eyes begin to feel so tire.

11. Softly and slowly opening them again now.

12. And close. Each time you open them it becomes more and more difficult. Heavier and heavier.

13. Feel the heaviness in your eyelids as you open them now.

14. And let them close down. Your eyelids are getting heavier and heavier, more and more tired with each number. That's fine. As it becomes more comfortable to just keep them closed, you can allow yourself to keep them closed now.

15. And open…so heavy…so tired.

16. And close them down again. So comfortable and relaxed. As you talk, your eyelids are becoming heavier and heavier, more and more relaxed now. Heavier and heavier with each number.

17. Feel the heaviness increasing now as you open them.

18. Let them close down again. Heavier and heavier now, so heavy, so tired, so relaxed, that's fine.

19. And open.

20. And closed. Your eyelids are so heavy now that it becomes increasingly difficult to open your eyes. Do not try to resist this. Just feel their heaviness and when it is more comfortable to keep your eyes closed, simply enjoy keeping them closed. That's fine.

21. And slowly open.

22. Now close them down. Just let them rest for a moment and enjoy feeling your eyes resting in their sockets. That's fine. Now that your eyes are closed, in a few short moments you will be so completely relaxed and comfortable that it will be easy for you to go into trance.

As you go into a trance you are still able to think thoughts. Thoughts can still be thought, but you do not have to think them. You may now like to imagine your thoughts floating away as though they are tied to a helium balloon that carries them effortlessly into the distance.

As you relax, wonder how it feels when you are so complete-ly relaxed that you lose awareness of your body; or perhaps what's it like when you are so comfortable, so snuggled, and warm that you can sink down deep into the comfort; or per-haps when you listen so intently to what someone is saying, everything else seems to disappear and you can imagine how it feels as all of your tensions melt away, allowing you to sink right down in the comfort.

To help you relax, imagine that you are outdoors on a won-derful summer's day. You find yourself in a safe and relaxing place where you are free to really relax and enjoy the environ-ment. Find a comfortable place to sit down where you can rest for a moment, perhaps leaning against a tree or a rock. That's fine.

You are safe and secure here, safe to relax completely no mat-ter how deeply you go into trance.

Mirror Technique

By the time you reach this section you will already be in a suggestible state, but the induction is not complete. It is now time to relax even further.

As you find your comfortable place to rest, begin to allow any tensions to simply melt away from you as though they are simply dripping out from your body and soaking down into the earth. To help you to relax, imagine that a small orb of positive relaxing energy is floating effortlessly above your head now—just hovering there waiting. You can imagine this orb any way you choose; you might see it as a light or a color, or perhaps you can simply sense its presence.

In a few moments, this orb of energy will slowly move through your body; as it does, every muscle that it touches instantly becomes twice as relaxed, allowing you to feel a soft heavy sweetness deep inside your muscles, causing your muscles to feel so very heavy, so limp and loose.

As you relax, you can imagine this orb is beginning its journey now, slowly lowering deeper and deeper as it eases gently through your scalp and deep, deep down to the very base of your brain—that's fine—relaxing you completely as it does.

As this energy begins to soak around the sides of your head, it sinks deep inside your ears, gliding around each side of your head now and gently soaking in and around your eyes, perhaps bringing wonderfully relaxing warmth or a cooling ease to your eyes as it does.

You can just take a few moments now to really relax all of those tiny muscles in and around your eyes. That's fine. Feel your brow ease as you relax your face, your eyes just resting in their sockets now, so comfortable, so easy, and so relaxed.

As you notice your eyes relaxing, this energy continues down through your cheeks and slowly into the muscles of your jaw. This wonderfully relaxed sensation is soaking deep into the bones of your jaw now, and as it does your jaw will hang limp and loose.

As you continue to relax, this sensation eases its way down into the powerful muscles of your neck, muscles that have been working so hard holding your heavy head upright all day. That's fine; just allow them to relax as this sensation gently spreads out across your shoulders. Notice how your shoulders can drop a little more with each relaxing outbreath until you feel quite free.

As you continue relaxing more and more, this wonderful

Richard Link

sensation eases its way deeper and deeper now—that's fine—deeper and deeper and just as you can go deeper and deeper into trance, this wonderful feeling can drift so deeply now so deeply down, soaking deep into your shoulders and slowly down your arms. Your arms are getting heavier and heavier as you relax, more and more relaxed, until they feel nice and limp and loose. That's good. The muscles of your arms are so relaxed now, like a handful of limp elastic bands. That's fine. As you enjoy these sensations, a gentle wave of relaxation begins at your shoulders and flows all the way down your back, taking you even deeper into trance.

Deeper and deeper into trance now, with no effort required at all. It is so easy to just relax and let it happen all by itself. Just like when you go to sleep at night; you just relax and let it happen all by itself. Trance is like that now. Go into trance and really enjoys the process as you relax deeper and deeper. That's fine.

As these feelings move down into your legs, you can imagine you have been running so fast for such a long time that you are so tired now, so tired that all you want to do is rest…and now you can rest—that's right—just allow your legs to relax. Now, relax and let go completely, feeling the tired heaviness taking you deeper and deeper.

Deepening Your Trance

The previous script will have put you into a light state of trance. At this stage, due to relaxation, you will be more susceptible to suggestion than in normal waking consciousness; however, to ensure the hypnosis is successful, you need to deepen the trance state. Deepening scripts create an association with moving in a downward direction and going into a deeper state of trance.

You are going to use a very simple script that is easy to learn here; it is very effective and many hypnotists use this method. Simply continue from where you left off with the following deepening instructions.

As a simple exercise, you have systematically relaxed your entire body and this has been very easy for you to do. Now it is time to go even deeper into trance. I would like you to imagine that you are standing at the top of an escalator. In a few moments you begin to count down from 10 to 1. this is a second, different count from that in the beginning.

When you say the number 10, you will step onto this escalator and as you count slowly down you will ride the escalator down until you reach the number 1 (one), where you will find yourself at the bottom of the escalator and step off.

Before you begin, I would like to inform you of the magical qualities of this imaginary escalator. This is the escalator of trance and the further down you ride, the deeper into trance you will go. As you count down slowly, each number that you count takes you even deeper into trance, and the deeper into trance you go, the more relaxed you become. The more relaxed you become, the deeper into trance you go. So as you stand at the top looking down, reach out now, ready to step onto this escalator of trance and…

10. Step onto the escalator now and hold the hand rail as you begin your journey, deeper and deeper into trance. Each number that you count takes you even deeper into trance and the further down the escalator you ride the deeper and deeper into trance you go.

9. Further down the escalator now, effortlessly gliding down into trance.

8. That's fine, each number taking you deeper and deeper into trance.

7. Comfortably gliding down into trance, so easily, so effortlessly, just relax and let it happen all by itself.

6. Deeper and deeper now.

5. Halfway down the escalator now, relaxing so easily, each number taking you deeper and deeper into trance.

4. Deeper and deeper, gliding effortlessly deeper and deeper down, becoming more and more relaxed with every number that passes.

3. As you approach the bottom of the escalator, you drift deeper and deeper into trance.

2. Almost at the bottom now and as you reach the bottom you can step off the escalator easily and naturally. The moment you step off the escalator, you fall into a deep, deep trance…and…

1. At the very bottom now as you step off the escalator, you become ten times as relaxed, going even deeper into trance.

The Transition

Now that you have completed the deepening process, you will be in a very suggestible state of trance.

To go even deeper into trance, you find yourself standing at the bottom of the escalator now. Just in front of you there is a bed, a very special bed, a bed of dreams. Should you clamber onto this bed you will instantly fall into a deep, deep sleep—but not the kind of sleep that you enter at night—a special kind of sleep, for this is the end of trance and when you clamber upon it you will enter a deep, deep hypnotic sleep.

Clamber upon the bed now and allow yourself to sink deeper and deeper into the soft comfort. As you sink into the comfort you fall into a deep, deep...SLEEEEEP!

That's fine...The kind of sleep where you can dream a special kind of hypnotic sleep, where you can dream that you are standing before a wonderfully comfortable bed, a magical bed, a bed that can realize your dreams. As you clamber upon this bed you fall into a deep, deep...SLEEEP!

The kind of sleep where you can dream...dream that you are going deeper and deeper now, deeper and deeper to...SLEEEP! A special kind of sleep where you can dream your dreams.

Trance Suggestions at This State in the Hypnosis Process

The transitional script that you have just learned makes it easy to follow through with your suggestions. This is the actual purpose of the hypnosis; without hypnotic suggestion you are doing nothing more than relaxing. Although this is incredibly beneficial in itself, it is unlikely to elicit positive life changes and certainly is not very entertaining. What you use the trance state for depends on your particular area of interest.

Perhaps one of the most important suggestions that you should include at this stage is that you will be able to get back into this state easily.

Trance Suggestions for Therapy

If you obey the three golden rules of therapy creation, you will be able to develop effective hypnotic scripts for almost any situation. The three essential rules of hypnotic suggestions are as follows:

1. Keep your suggestions positive.

2. Keep your suggestions in the present tense.

3. Test everything by future pacing before you make any changes—that is, image what the future would look like, what kind of consequences you might have to face, if the situation you are working on were healed.

By adhering to these simple rules, you avoid some of the common pitfalls of hypnotherapy.

For example, if you are treating yourself for smoking, a statement such as "I will stop smoking in 2 weeks" would break the first two rules. But you make a similar suggestion with the statement, "In 2 weeks time, I am a non-smoker." This keeps the suggestion positively focused and in the present tense. It might appear at first glance to be in the future tense, but the statement "I am a non-smoker" is set in the present. This will have an affect on how your subconscious mind accepts and acts upon it.

Getting Out of the Trance

One of the most commonly accepted misconceptions of trance is that it is possible to become "stuck" in hypnosis. This simply is not true. It is no more possible to get stuck in hypnosis than it is to get stuck in normal sleep.

Having said that, you still need to know the correct way to wake up. The following script should serve you well. The golden rule here is to not wake up too abruptly and to always wake up in a good mood! Just as you progressively reduced your tempo during the induction, it is now time to increase the tempo and volume as you run through the wake-up script. Be enthusiastic and make your voice vibrant and exciting as you speak to yourself.

Start counting from 1 to 5. When you reach the number 5, you will be completely awake and feel absolutely fantastic. With each number that you count, you become more and more alert until on the number 5 you open your eyes and are wide awake.

Say to yourself the following:

1. I am beginning to awake now, aware of my own voice and the room around me.

2. I am waking from the trance state feeling fantastic, bringing with me all that I have learned.

3. I am aware of my body now and the position of my arms and legs.

Stretch your arms now as you begin to open your eyes, feeling refreshed and excited about your trance experience. With eyes open and wide awake, you are feeling fantastic! Well done!

Like anything else, if you don't practice or at least do some of the techniques on fairly regular basis, you won't get much out of them. I, however, sincerely trust you will do all of the necessary exercises to conquer your depression.

Your beliefs become your
Thoughts
Your thoughts become your
Words
Your words become your
Actions
Your actions become your
Habits
Your habits become your
Values

Misery to Bliss

Your Choice: Reach Your Pinnacle or Stay in Your Pit

Now it is up to YOU and only YOU. Only through YOUR persistent work will you reach the pinnacle. Live your dreams, reach your goals. YOU have the tools, the methods, and the directions. Follow this plan and I guarantee you will REACH YOUR PINNACLE! The only way for you to change your life is to take action NOW. Live your dreams! And do it NOW. No more excuses. No longer will you allow depression to hold you back. A new you will be released. Just think, you will be able to dream and live again. A new world will open before your eyes; you will see all of your hopes and dreams. Your friends will be friendlier, your world fresher, and your touch, smell, taste, sight, and hearing will be alive.

Using my course, you will be able to help members in your family defeat depression as well as myriad of other negative emotions and feelings. Here are two short testimonials I have received and want to share with you. You can see below that the value of my course is already paying off for two people. They had all but given up hope. But after using my Misery to Bliss course, here's what they said:

> *The sooner Richard gets his program Misery to Bliss out, the sooner will people be given the most wonderful course there is. He in fact used me as a guinea pig. Words can't express what it has done for me. NO Depression. I feel great*
>
> —Peter K.

> *The program Misery to Bliss is an absolute must for people who not only suffer from emotional issues, but you can use the program as a preventative program from getting trapped with emotional negative problems.*
>
> —Irene Katsis, Melbourne

It doesn't get much better than that. Following my Misery to Bliss, I can guarantee you will conquer your depression!

Break the shackles of hopelessness and dejection. Until now, you have merely existed and may not remember how to actually live. You will need to adjust to the new you, a stronger person. It will be like looking at the world through magic glasses. Everything will be brighter, deeper, more colorful. You will be alive, able to experience and taste life again. Your health will return and you will be much more alert. What a pleasure it will be for you to feel your happiness return, and how your happiness has touched all of the lives around you.

You will experience new joys and hopes and dreams as your new life develops.

The home study course is an amazing opportunity. It shows how to drive depression out of your life permanently. This may become a struggle for some, because you must meet the root causes of your depression head on. I explain systematically what methods to use and help you select the best path to follow.

You can use my home study course as a handy, readily available resource. Use it as a reference to help your loved ones overcome their depression. Put what you are learning in this book into action. You know you will not do as well on your own as you will with guidance.

I have presented a number of techniques to help you go from Misery to Bliss. Freedom from depression is now possible and within your grasp. You will have the tools to take you from the pit to the pinnacle. This will truly provide you an escape from depression, something you are searching for and need. Imagine the impact on your family and friends: no more dark days.

You will no longer be hiding in the shadows and will finally achieve a release from the cycles of despair and despondency. They will see a new you, very much alive, able to return to a normal state of life. Your life will be turned around.

Now you have read and implemented the procedures and process *From the Pit to the Pinnacle, Conquer Your Depression in 20 Minutes a Day and Awaken Your Bliss.* The processes in this book will be the best investment of 20 minutes a day you could make. As demonstrated by Ann and John in their two separate problems, you can select the right solutions to your own individual attacks of depression. After following the steps in my home study course, your total satisfaction is personally guaranteed by myself, Richard Link.

Yes, I know it is difficult to believe, but I teach YOU how to master your mind, changing your story to change your life and your world. Act now because you are literally one step away from returning to your life and dreams. Your dream drives you into action. Your challenges do not set you back for long. As you grow and become stronger, you realize how to tap into the power of your pain, learn how to recognize signs of your depression coming toward you, and discover how to banish negative thoughts. You too will feel the happiness, joy, and anticipation of living a full life every day!

About the Author

Richard Link, the founder and director of Mindeze, began his career as a secondary school teacher after graduating with a Bachelor of Science with a major in Physiology and Paramedic Studies and a Diploma of Education from Melbourne University. Richard has attained diplomas in Applied Physiology from the International Institute of Applied Physiology (1989), Kinesiology (with Dr. Bruce Dew in 1984), and Qigong (with Jack Lin in 1984). He has honed his skills by attending numerous other workshops in Natural Health Therapies.

Richard practiced Kinesiology for 22 years and later started teaching Qigong. About 15 years ago, he discovered a technique he named "Emotional Mindeze Therapy" (EMT). The effectiveness of the technique even surprised Richard himself. After five years of seeing positive results, Richard could not deny EMT's ability to help patients and started to apply the technique professionally. It has been successfully improving the quality of life for many patients ever since.

At Mindeze, Richard runs workshops, seminars, and practitioner training courses, and conducts private consultations. Richard is also a much sought-after speaker, both nationally and internationally, and continues to instruct Qigong.

Richard is available to give presentations, workshops, and seminars. In fact, he gives free information presentations to interested groups or organizations. If you wish, he can speak to you personally. He can also participate in your teleseminar, and is available for interviews in any media setting.

Richard is passionate about reaching out to as many people as he can, to research and develop natural health techniques for the health and well-being to each individual.

You can contact Richard via email at:

richard@mindeze.com

His website:

www.mindeze.com

You can also get some free "stuff" here.

Works he has authored can be found here:

www.fromthepittothepinnacle.com

www.free-your-spirit-heal-your-life.com

Programs that conquer your depression:

www.miserytobliss.com

Programs that enhance learning:

www.mindezegym.com

See 1stWorld Books at:

www.1stWorldPublishing.com

See our classic collection at:

www.1stWorldLibrary.com